DESIGN WORKS

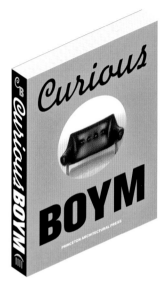

This book belongs to

_____

Published by
Princeton Architectural Press
37 East Seventh Street
New York, New York 10003

For a free catalog of books,
call 1.800.722.6657.
Visit our Web site at
www.papress.com.

©2002 Princeton Architectural Press
and Constantin Boym

Library of Congress Cataloging-in-Publication Data

Boym, Constantin.
Curious Boym : design works / written by Constantin
Boym ; essays by Peter Hall, Steven Skov Holt.
p. cm.
ISBN 1-56898-353-0 (alk. paper)
1. Design, Industrial. 2. Boym, Constantin. I. Title.
TS171.4 .B72 2002
745.2'092—dc21
2002008362

CURIOUS BOYM
Design Works

*C*B

Written by
Constantin Boym

Essays by
Peter Hall
Steven Skov Holt

Book Design by
karlssonwilker inc.,
New York

Published by
Princeton Architectural Press,
New York

Designer as Curious George

Thanks to our five-year-old son Bobby, we have been introduced recently to a fascinating world of children's literature. In one of Bobby's books, we met our unlikely role model, Curious George, a cute little monkey who traveled from the jungle to live in the exciting modern world. He is driven by curiosity to play and experiment with elements of his daily environment. He finds new uses for familiar objects, invents different ways of doing things, and tests the limits of materials and objects. Many of his experiments do not work, and he routinely gets in trouble, but occasionally he reaps praise or a medal.

This sounds a lot like a designer's life. After all, the role of the designer today is to be on a continuing lookout, to detect all the intangible waves of emerging needs, trends, and desires, and then, as Tom Ford of Gucci puts it, to "try to give people what they want before they know they want it." This is the way our studio works. Our projects reflect on everyday aspects of the American lifestyle and landscape, on familiar things that often pass unnoticed because of their very proximity.

The diabolical nature of our profession is that, to be successful, a designer's very personal vision has to be wanted by everyone. Whereas in art a personal expression is the most important and praised quality, in design, companies prefer a middle ground— products that conform to as many different tastes as possible. The same corporate design continues to spread around the globe. While the best of American culture, from music to fashion to visual arts, samples the creative cultural margins with curiosity and humor, design remains a largely self-contained discipline.

And yet, as Tibor Kalman has urged, we have to "find the cracks in the wall." The work in this book highlights a few clients with a vision, who were able to avoid the common mold, allowing for some unusual products and environments to come forth. When we run out of such clients, we take the matters in our own hands. The game is not over. We are eager to go on.

Constantin Boym
Laurene Leon Boym
2002

*Boym Studio graphic identity,
designed by Alexander Gelman
in 1994*

THE DISCREET CHARM OF THE ORDINARY
Peter Hall

Design, as the Boym Studio is acutely aware, has always had
a complex relationship with mass manufacturing. In its recently
completed exhibition design, Alliance of Art and Industry:
Toledo Designs for a Modern America, the studio presents
a wry, ambivalent framework to address the commercial roots
of the industrial design profession. Born during the Depression,
design was sold essentially by its pioneers—Walter Dorwin
Teague, Raymond Loewy, and Harold Van Doren—as an extension
of advertising, a means of boosting the sales of goods. "The
product had to be made to sell itself," explained George Nelson in
Fortune magazine of February 1934. "Designers were called in."

Yet as the profession matured, this model came to seem
too limited. Nelson complained in *Fortune* in 1949 that "it has
been the glib assumption of most manufacturers and designers
that the prime function of industrial design is the creation of
added sales appeal." He argued that this was a "temporary and
superficial" aspect of a designer's activity, far less important than
the job of reintegrating a society shattered by new technology,
and bringing "cheaper and better goods for all." As designer
styling came to be associated with product obsolescence,
stronger voices of dissent emerged, from Vance Packard's
1957 book *The Hidden Persuaders* and Victor Papanek's *Design
for the Real World.* "There are professions more harmful than
industrial design, but only a very few of them," argued Papanek,
calling for a "frugal sensuousness" in design, combining
"common sense and aesthetic excellence."

For the Boym Studio, design is about treading the line between
the sales curve and their artistic goals. "It's a difficult
profession," says Constantin Boym, "because you combine

personal expression with something that has to sell. Our design career has been a struggle between two poles—what we wanted to say and what the market needs." Like their forebear, George Nelson, Constantin and Laurene Leon Boym's approach begins not with an identifiable, saleable style, but with a curiosity about process. For Nelson, the questioning approach yielded a collection of innovative ideas—from the storage wall to the ball clock. For the Boyms it has produced an eclectic and ingenious array of projects that address functional, social, and philosophical questions.

The Boyms' perspective comes to some extent from a frame of reference outside the American design profession. Constantin trained as an architect in Moscow and Milan, and Laurene, though trained in the United States, has the fairly rare position of a woman in a notoriously male-dominated profession. "There aren't many woman industrial designers," she says, "because manufacturers just don't respect them."

Constantin Boym, who was born in Moscow in 1955, was one of the last Russian Jews to defect from the Soviet Union through a bureaucratic loophole in the Iron Curtain. As a student, Boym had experienced the stultifying effects of the Communist regime on creativity, when he was part of a team whose design of a "theater of the future" won an international prize that included a two-month internship in Paris. The Soviet authorities inevitably forbade the trip and Boym, along with his parents, saw that in the Soviet Union, as he puts it, "There was no hope trying to excel." A 1975 human rights accord allowing Russian Jews to emigrate to the West presented Boym with an opportunity to escape the unexciting prospects of a lifetime's employment as a

Brezhnev Clock, from the collection A Short History of Time, one-off made in 1989

Pin for a Berlin exhibition of Russian-American artists Komar & Melamid, designed in 1988. The design quotes the shape of the Soviet Army decoration given for the liberation of Berlin in 1945.

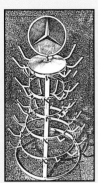

Reliquaries of the Twentieth
Century, project at Domus
Academy, 1984

state architect in an office of thousands. The emigration process
was risky, however, as those who applied were effectively
showing disloyalty to the State; friends routinely broke off
contact for risk of appearing to sympathize, and applicants were
obliged to wait in a state of limbo for approval to leave. The
loophole was closed after war broke out in Afghanistan, but not
before Constantin and his wife at the time, author Svetlana
Boym, were let out. By 1981, they were living in Boston.

Boym's shift from architecture to product design was set into
motion a few years later with his decision to leave a position at
the Boston architecture firm Graham Gund to enroll in the
Masters program at the newly founded Domus Academy in Milan.
At the time, Milan was the undisputed design capital of the West,
and in the grip of the creative frenzy of the postmodern
Memphis movement.

Arriving in the city in 1984, Boym experienced the pioneering
hands-on, apprenticeship-style teaching methods of the Domus
Academy, and the energy and culture of the Milan designers who
visited the school. These included architect and theorist Andrea
Branzi, a pioneer of the Radical Design movement, whose work in
the early 1980s included efforts to transfigure everyday consumer
objects into objects of aesthetic contemplation with the
application of color and pattern. Radical Design paved the way
for the Memphis design group, whose founder, Ettore Sottsass,
Jr., had worked in the United States with George Nelson before
returning to Italy in the 1960s and embarking on a series of
ceramics that sought, through symbolism, to "decondition"
people and provide a launching point for meditation and self-
discovery. Memphis revoked the Fordist goals of a standardized
design for all in favor of batch-produced, computer-aided

manufacturing that could satisfy the varying cultural values of different consumer groups. Its language, famously, was derived from ancient iconography, American diner vernacular, and everything in between.

After ten months in the vicinity of designers like Branzi, Boym became convinced that "all ideas that could be expressed in architecture could be expressed in objects." Branzi, he adds, "taught me that design is first and foremost an expression of a certain idea. The shape and quantity is only as good as the idea."

The importance of Branzi's dictum began to manifest itself in Boym's work a few years later. He reluctantly returned to the United States, after a short period working for designer Alessandro Mendini, to deal with the dissolution of his marriage to Svetlana. Following advice from peers, he moved to New York, where he designed a Memphis-influenced furniture collection under the company name Nota Bene. The late-1980s recession prompted Boym to close the firm in 1988, though not before he had made a number of useful connections in the New York design and manufacturing communities. Boym Studio came into being the following year with the Recycle project.

Like the later American Plumbing vase, which Boym simply adapted from a piece of white plastic PVC plumbing, the Recycle project incorporated a wink to Marcel Duchamp's readymades and a nod to Boym's Italian education. By setting banal bottles, glasses, and plates inside wood, metal, and concrete frames, Recycle literally framed the everyday within a new context. Garnering considerable press attention, the project foreshadowed a wider appreciation in design and literature for unnoticed and anonymous objects, as investigated in books like Henry Petroski's

First chair design, 1985

Nota Bene furniture collection, designed and manufactured in Italy for distribution in the United States, 1986

Wizard of Oz, a collection of domestic appliances designed in 1992

top to bottom: Cowardly Lion Electric Tea Kettle; Dorothy Toaster; Scarecrow Crockpot

The Evolution of Useful Things of 1992. It also established the Boym Studio on a similar trajectory to those of designers Jasper Morrison, Ron Arad, and, later, Konstantin Grcic, who began their first design investigations with found objects.

Laurene Leon Boym's development as a designer followed a contrasting but not unrelated path. Born in Manhattan in 1964, Leon studied fine art at the School of Visual Arts and won a scholarship to study for a Masters in Industrial Design at the Pratt Institute. Her fine art thesis at the School of Visual Arts was a critique of consumerism, and as a Masters student at Pratt she developed a series of domestic appliances based on characters from the *Wizard of Oz*. Like the Memphis designs that influenced Constantin, the Oz family emerged as designers began exploring the possibilities of form liberated from its functional duties. With miniaturized circuitry, toasters, kettles, coffee makers, and washing machines were increasingly alike on the inside, and the designer, freed from the obligation to simply encase bulky mechanisms, was able to explore new semantic possibilities. In Leon's case, this raised the opportunity to design forms that avoided the standard tropes of speed, ease of use, or spatial efficiency in favor of a narrative approach more in keeping with women's oral storytelling traditions. "I was interested in how women relate to objects and the history of consumerist design," she says.

Developed with the encouragement of Leon's advisor, designer Tucker Viemeister, who subsequently hired her to work briefly at Smart Design, the Oz family included a Scarecrow Crockpot, a Wicked Witch of the East blender, a Good Witch Glenda ice cream maker, and a Cowardly Lion tea kettle. The collection became a star feature of the Cooper-Hewitt National Design Museum's 1993 exhibition Mechanical Brides: Women and Machines from Home to Office, where curator Ellen Lupton juxtaposed their characterful forms against an American tradition of products designed and marketed by men towards women. Amid the phones, vacuum cleaners, washing machines, and irons that sought to appeal to—and to an extent resemble—the women expected to use them, the Oz family issued a derisive laugh. They did not pretend to offer liberation from domestic servitude, but they did draw attention to the cultural uses and meanings of the designed world. As Lupton argued hopefully in the exhibition catalog, "Reading the social text of the designed environment is a step toward achieving power and choice in daily life."

The Boyms met in 1988 at Parsons School of Design, where Constantin was teaching furniture design and Laurene was taking a continuing education class. Their first collaboration was an edible pencil designed for a competition organized by the Industrial Designers Society of America. Baked in cookie dough, the pencil won first prize, followed by more press attention and an invitation from Alessi, the Italian manufacturer, to Laurene to participate in a new series of designs created by women. To the Boyms' quiet amusement, Alessi deemed that an appropriate object for women to design was the serving container. Laurene responded with a vessel inspired by the lowly form of the Dixie cup, enlarged to proportions unimaginable to all but the thirstiest fast-food consumer.

An important idea in relation to the Boyms' work is Andrea Branzi's postmodern contention that products born in the new

The Boyms' first collaboration—Edible Pencil—won a first prize at the IDSA Competition for a New Writing Instrument in 1989

Dixie Cup for Alessi's Memory Containers, designed in 1990

The Cheapest Lamp Possible, designed at Domus Academy in 1985, remade for Gallery 91 in New York in 1997

market economy—as opposed to the earlier political economy—could no longer be justified as part of the advance of modernity, industrialization, or democracy. "The [design] project is a tautological creative act," argued Branzi in *Learning from Milan,* "a pure linguistic and economic invention, which sometimes tries to respond to a demand from the market and at others invents a market for itself." Since 1988, when Branzi's book was written, several design groups, including the Boym Studio, have come to the conclusion that they must, indeed, invent a market.

The Boyms' closest counterparts are Droog Design, the Netherlands-based collective launched in Milan in 1994 by curators and organizers Renny Ramakers and Gijs Bakker. The Droog statute, according to an early statement, was to solicit and promote "original ideas and clear concepts which have been shaped in a wry, no-nonsense manner." Droog also became known for embracing a reversal of the designer's role, from seeking to create products that would become obsolete, to espousing long-lasting products from unexpected resources. Indeed, one Droog designer and sometime Boym collaborator Marcel Wanders has argued, à la Branzi, that in an age of excessive consumerism objects should be "made with love."

Droog, Wanders, and the Boym Studio have independently arrived at the same premise that, for self-generated projects at least, the designer must take charge of production. Early encouragement to this end came from Tibor Kalman, who suggested to Constantin that real challenges do not come from clients, but from designers themselves. The surprise financial success of the resulting miniature buildings series, Missing Monuments and Buildings of Disaster, gave the Boyms the final financial incentive

Rubber Band Clock, a prototype, designed in 2000. Six stretched rubber bands make up the dial.

to form Handy, a company with a distinctly antiestablishment rationale. "The bottom line for Handy is that the project should be crazy enough so that it's useless to approach any manufacturer with it," says Constantin. "The Buildings of Disaster, for example, would be kicked out of the door by a manufacturer."

For Laurene, Handy has provided an outlet for developing the character-based design ideas first explored in her Oz family. Rugs and giant pillows imprinted with cartoon-like graphics, including a rug featuring a loveable sitting dog rendered in glow-in-the-dark dyes, are among the first products to emerge from the company. This use of exaggerated graphics as a design device has its direct forebear in the "supergraphics" of the seminal postmodern architect Venturi, Scott Brown & Associates, who famously noted the transformational semiotic effects of advertising signs on the generic "decorated sheds" of Las Vegas. Supergraphics first found their way into the Boyms' work in a showroom designed for furniture maker Vitra at the Neocon trade fair in Chicago in 1999. They reach their interactive apogee with an upcoming line of products developed for Flos. As Laurene sees it, Handy "sits half way between craft and design," with the expressed goal of evoking a sense of "fun and joy."

Despite the presence of alternative practices like Droog, Wanders, and the Boyms, public perception of design today is still remarkably obsessed with style. The most prominent names in the media in 2002 were strongly associated with distinctive styles: Marc Newson, Philippe Starck, and Karim Rashid. Murray Moss, owner of the Moss store, Manhattan's unofficial downtown design museum, argues that style is irrelevant to the Boyms' design mission. The entire Boym output, he contends, is inherently antimaterialistic, being rooted in their appreciation of

Sheep in the City, animal rug for Handy, 2001

the souvenir. Material, form, and style are secondary to the idea in a souvenir. "They see everything as a souvenir," he says. "Their things are souvenirs of their ideas, their ideas made tangible. In art, an unflattering way one could characterize them is as trash artists. They work with garbage, or humble materials. They're not into carbon fiber. Their focus is not on the richness of materials—it's much more conceptual."

Moss's argument distinguishes the Boyms' work from that of some of their Droog counterparts, like Hella Jongerius, whose methodology often begins with new materials and technologies. It also suggests that Boym design is really less about things and more about a way of seeing. This may explain why the Boyms' exhibition work is the medium in which Constantin and Laurene's discrete approaches seem to converge with the most ease. The first goal of Alliance of Art and Industry: Toledo Designs for a Modern America was to prevent the collection of vintage everyday objects from looking like an antiques market or yard sale. The Boym approach was to single out the objects like readymades, in sparse arrangements and odd juxtapositions. In the transportation gallery, a collection of children's toys with teardrop-shaped fenders travel in an opposite direction than the adult vehicles—the Jeep and its descendants the Wagoneer and Cherokee—as if in defiant parody. The introduction of supergraphics, including a two-dimensional continuation of a hopelessly ambitious 1940s "kitchen of the future," frame the artifacts with the gently ironic perspective of a twenty-first-century observer.

Museums typically collect and present objects for their historical or symbolic value—in other words, according to criteria that have to do with something other than commerce. Since the original

Intelligent Souvenir, project for Things That Think at MIT Media Lab, 1995. These souvenirs would provide information about a monument, including not only the historical past but also a background of sounds, noises, and other sensations. On top of this, the owner would be able to add personal impressions, thoughts and greetings.

Plastic Memories, installation for Authentics at the Milan Furniture Fair in 1998

context of much product design is a retail environment, the Boyms' ability to recontexualize artifacts becomes a valuable curatorial weapon. At the Cooper-Hewitt National Design Museum's 1994 show Packaging the New, the Boyms, confronted with the stately interior of the museum, called a double bluff and constructed mock supermarket shelves to reiterate the curator's critical account of consumerism. The 1996 A Personal Gathering exhibit at the Wichita Art Museum of the vast, eclectic art collection of local entrepreneur William I. Koch took a similar about-face and grouped the artworks like commodities, according to their subject matter—women, warfare, ships, and landscapes, for example—rather than by painter or period.

Objects removed from their natural environment often become replete with mnemonic connotations, and this, ultimately, helps explain the extraordinary resonance of some of the Boym Studio's work. The theme of human memory is implicit, even in such mainstream projects as the Boyms' collection of plastic storage containers designed for Authentics, which recalled the glass cubes of Bauhaus designer Wilhelm Wagenfeld. With the American Plumbing vase, the chair made of industrial strapping tape, and the clock made of TV antenna in the form of Nelson's Ball Clock, part of the appeal of the materials and the readymade is familiarity. "There is something reassuring in forms and shapes that already exist," says Constantin. The object, as if through alchemy, is transformed into something vile or something sublime, depending on how we read it. Coming from a studio rooted in commercial practice, this is no small feat.

Packaging the New, an exhibition design for the Cooper-Hewitt National Design Museum, received a Federal Design Achievement Award in 1994

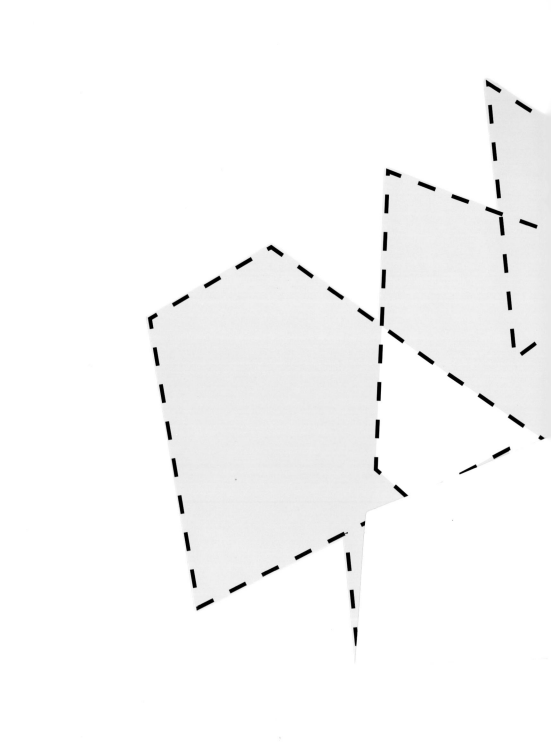

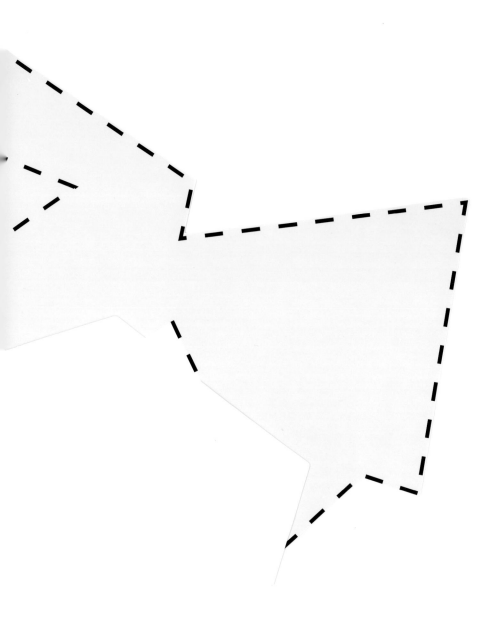

Flea market in New York City

"If we wish to grasp the full
expressive capacity of the
apparently mundane swirl of
things all around us, we need to
begin by approaching everyday
life itself as a continually
unfolding masterpiece."
—Dan Cameron

RECYCLE

Boym Studio's first independent work, the Recycle project
outlined many directions still relevant for our design work
today.

The project approached the theme of recycling (at the
time, a largely unexplored concept) in cultural rather than
environmental terms. It aimed to recycle the aesthetic
and cultural significance of everyday things. Every work in
the collection utilized at least one common object, a thing
so familiar as to pass virtually unnoticed in people's daily
use. Over forty objects from the Recycle project were
exhibited in the end of 1988 at Gallery 91 in Soho, at the
time an important New York showcase of new design.

The appeal of the familiar goes beyond borders or trends.

From top:
Surrealist objects (René Magritte, Personal Values, 1952) ©2002 C. Herscovici, Brussels/Artists Rights Society (ARS), New York

American Pop Art (Jasper Johns, Flashlight, 1960) ©Jasper Johns/Licensed by VAGA, New York

Le Corbusier's interior of monastery kitchen (La Tourette, 1957)

Droog Design (Rody Graumans, 85 Lamps, 1993)

All objects had elaborate frames made of plywood, concrete, or metal built around them, outlining their shapes and elevating them onto a different typological level. For example, a wine glass would turn into a vase, a plate into a fruit bowl, a bunch of office supplies into a desk organizer. Above all, frames served to estrange the objects from their conventional contexts. Framing was closely related to defamiliarization, a concept articulated back in the 1920s by the Russian Literary Formalists. Their oft-quoted motto, "The old and habitual must be spoken of as if it were new and unusual," effectively describes the entire project.

Much speculation was made about the "Russian origins" of the Recycle project. Perhaps my growing up in Russia conditioned a certain "outsider's" point of view, enabling me to reflect on things that others would barely notice. New York flea markets looked as exciting as exhibitions of Surrealist objects. American Pop Art was an important inspiration, even though our soup cans were stripped of their Campbell's labels, as if returning the objects to their pure essential state.

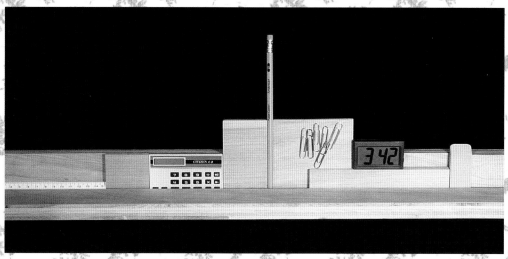

"Two things about the Russians:
they serve vodka at gallery
openings, and they're good at
seeing things we don't see."
—Karrie Jacobs, Interview

"Perhaps only a Russian who
studied in Italy could see
America—its post-industrial
strangeness and its
transcendental beauty—with
fresh eyes. Boym looked at our
supermarket shelves and had
a vision."
—Steven Holt, Metropolitan
Home

The Recycle project was favorably, if not ironically, received by critics. In 1990, an irreverent interview with Karrie Jacobs appeared on the pages of *Interview* magazine. "What kind of guy puts garbage in a frame?" wondered the article. Boym's curious design reputation gradually started to spread.

Interiors of the house in
Vinalhaven, Maine, the birthplace
of Searstyle

SEARSTYLE

In the summer of 1991 we spent a week on the island of Vinalhaven, Maine, in a house rented by a duo of conceptual Russian-American artists, Komar & Melamid, and their families. One night, on instigation of Alex Melamid, we all experienced a kind of aesthetic revelation. The nondescript domestic interior of that Maine house, complete with wood grain paneling, brown shag carpeting, and traditional furniture, suddenly revealed its powerful strangeness. We realized with amazement how this uniquely American vernacular has failed to find any reflection in contemporary design language.

This was the beginning of the Searstyle project. It is said that when Franklin D. Roosevelt was asked what American book he would like to place in the hands of every Russian, his selection was not really a book. It was the Sears catalog. For most of the twentieth century, Sears stood as a symbol of America, of all good, practical, dependable things this country has created and sold. As the decades rolled on, Sears became associated with symbols of a different kind: those of kitsch, banality, and suburbia. With the Searstyle project we attempted to bring this long-ignored American visual language back into contemporary design.

We discovered that the Sears catalog offered a selection of furniture components as replacement parts for their own pieces. We ordered and shipped these parts to our studio, where we put them together in new, unexpected juxtapositions within specially designed structural frames. The altered functions and unusual proportional relationships brought the Sears aesthetics back into the present, with a knowing wink to and warm embrace of the familiar.

In February 1992, Searstyle furniture had a first public presentation at Fullscale Gallery in New York. At the same time, Komar & Melamid exhibited Searstyle art at the Ronald Feldman Fine Arts gallery.

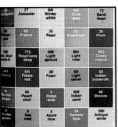

Pages from Sears catalog, 1993. Furniture parts (seats, backs, and frames) are all offered separately as replacements for damaged or worn parts—an economical and practical measure. Dozens of available colors with names like Rose Dust and Royal Blue Mist promise heavenly rest.

Many pieces in the collection were devoted to seating.
Americans like to sit softly, and the Sears catalog offers a great
many "cushions and pads to fill your every need." Our favorite
was the winged bedrest, a unique American invention commonly
used for reading, eating, and watching TV in bed. Popularly
called "husband" because of its characteristic hugging gesture,
this pillow provided material for the most acclaimed pieces of
the Searstyle collection. For a chaise longue (top left), we used
two sets of replacement parts, all combined in a single
composition.

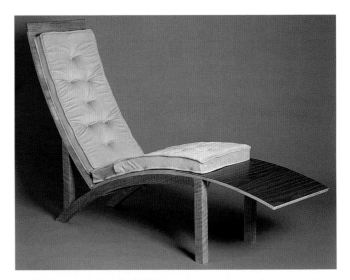

Top to bottom:
Woodgrain on an American car

Contract textile used for
Searstyle sofa (designer
unknown)

Wood by Komar & Melamid
(1991)

Discovery by René Magritte
(1928) ©2002 C. Herscovici,
Brussels/Artists Rights Society
(ARS), New York

Woodgrain Formica, a familiar material that combines
technological sophistication, economic benefits, and cultural
values of the traditional American home, was widely used in
the Searstyle furniture collection. The wood surface appeals to
the American pioneer spirit. On the other hand, Freud found a
connection between the grain of wood and the idea of woman,
the mother. (It is not by chance that the Formica advertisers
have always targeted woodgrain laminates to their male
customers.) With its reassuring presence, woodgrain signifies
the home itself, exuding a maternal aura of domesticity. It
covers American television sets and air conditioners to
domesticate these appliances, to ease their powerful presence
in bedrooms and living rooms. It was not easy to pick out three
woodgrain laminates for the project out of the forty-one
varieties offered by Formica.

By 1993, Searstyle furniture was featured in over 100 publications in American and international press, not all of them entirely flattering. Even the critics who praised the furniture as a witty and ironic commentary on American taste often missed an important pragmatic point of the project. After the design exuberance of the 1980s, Searstyle was envisioned as a concrete proposal aimed at bringing common sense, modesty, and economy of means into the tired world of furniture design. We even manufactured election-style buttons touting "Searstyle for the 90's!" and distributed them to the public at openings and design events. In the meantime, Sears, Roebuck & Co. (who never authorized or sponsored the project) kept an indifferent silence, despite the prodding of some design journalists.

In 1994, German design impresario Mattias Dietz joined forces with famed Barcelona retailer Fernando Amat to bring Searstyle furniture to Europe. Their show in Frankfurt took place on the site of the world's largest furniture fair. The room-size exhibition was allotted a huge space, which we surrounded with a forest of Formica flags. An original sign specially made in New York, "Everything Must Go," served as the metaphysical title of the installation. An exhibition at Barcelona's Vinçon Gallery (right) had a more introverted feel. A copy of the Sears catalog was displayed for the public to peruse at both locations on a special pedestal. In Germany, the birthplace of kitsch, the design public immediately understood and appreciated the project. Audiences in Barcelona and Paris, with their highly refined aesthetic sensibilities, had a harder time relating to the unusual "brute" shapes.

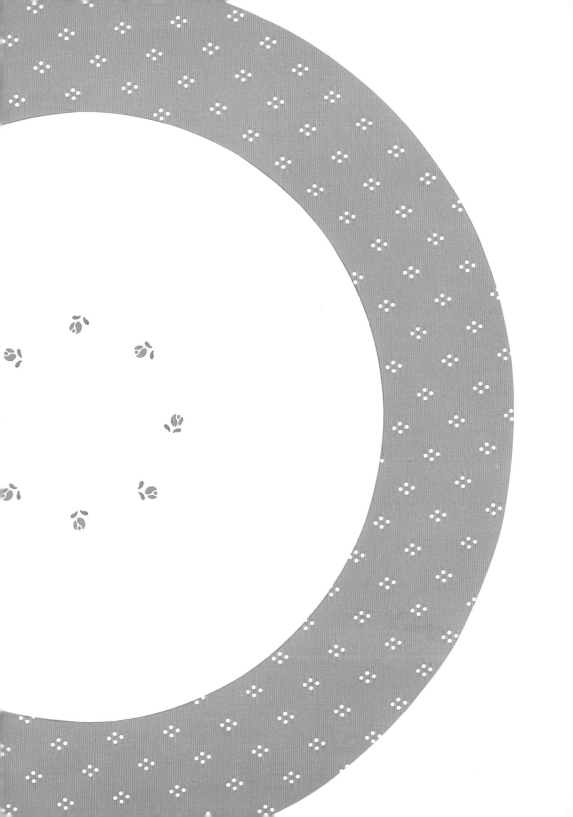

Further developments of the Searstyle collection took us into
the design of tableware. We created patterns of Searsware
plates from adhesive vinyl film, normally used for lining kitchen
shelves and drawers. Like the furniture, these plates combined
the reassuring familiar feel with the ironic detachment of
modernity. Several manufacturers considered producing
Searsware, but eventually all declined. Of all our designs, only
a set of coffee mugs (next page) was issued in a limited edition
by Authentics in Germany.

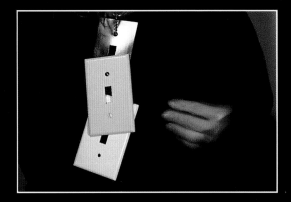

In a strange twist of fate, the Sears catalog itself was terminated in 1993 as part of Sears, Roebuck & Co.'s attempt to curb their slipping profits.

Between 1992 and 1994, we applied the idea of Searstyle to
many different fields, from jewelry and flatware to clothing and
architecture. We even concocted and tested a Searstyle cocktail
(mix equal parts of vodka and prune juice, add ice).

However, Searstyle as a total movement had fallen short of our
expectations. The furniture never went into production, and
only a number of selected pieces were made to order. The most
notable commission came from Philippe Starck, who specified
a set of chairs and sofas for the lounge of his restaurant Teatriz
in Mexico City. Designs for many other items have remained
at the proposal stage. We did notice that the grunge movement,
which emerged in American music and fashion in the 1990s,
found inspiration in the cultural sources we explored
in Searstyle.

Sidewalks of the downtown
Meat Market, New York City

STRAP FURNITURE

In 1996, Boym Studio moved into the Meat Market district, an old area in downtown Manhattan where meat is packaged to supply most of the New York restaurants. One of the last remaining areas to retain the gritty character of old New York, it soon started to affect our work. Every morning we would walk by heaps of discarded packaging materials that, like spontaneous industrial collages, would stimulate ideas and inspiration. Specifically, the polypropylene strapping tape used for securing cartons appeared to be an excellent material for experimentation.

Strapping tape for sale

We obtained strapping tape along with odd-looking special tools for tensioning, sealing, and cutting through industrial catalogs. Each strand of tape is designed to withstand the weight of at least three hundred pounds, hence the idea to weave it into a sitting surface seemed guaranteed to work. In the final designs, a web of strapping tape is applied onto a wooden framework reminiscent of an archetypal American easy chair. The result presents an alternative to traditional upholstery: lightweight, three-dimensional, and seemingly very complex (even though it was fairly straightforward to make). Steven Skov Holt described it as "cushions of air encased in a network of lines."

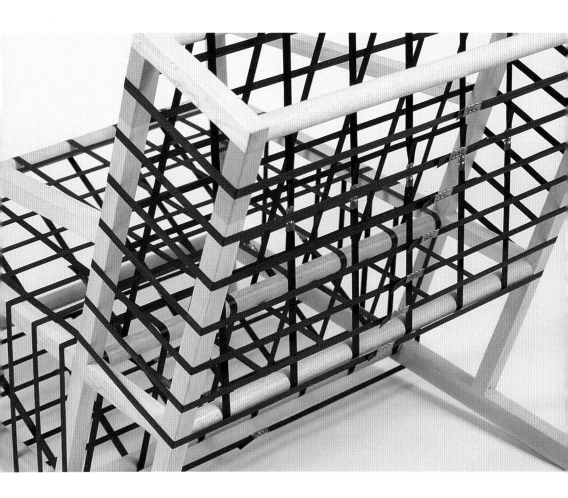

We applied strapping to other furniture types in addition to seating. In a prototype for a mirror, the tape not only held the sandwiched materials together, but also allowed for a casual display of photos and memos. A furniture piece for a lobby combined functions of a table and a small bench. The strands of tape supported stacks of magazines and could offer an informal sitting surface.

In May 1999, Strap Furniture was presented to the New York public in the exhibition Conversation Pieces, along with furniture by Lloyd Schwan. In 2000, fragments from the collection were selected for Cooper-Hewitt's National Design Triennial; the Strap Chair was one of the most publicized pieces of the show. For the exhibition, we suggested an innovative architectural application of strapping tape, an attempt to "update" the grand stair of Cooper-Hewitt's Carnegie mansion. This minimal, completely removable intervention, realized only in part, proved very effective for visually connecting different floors of the exhibition.

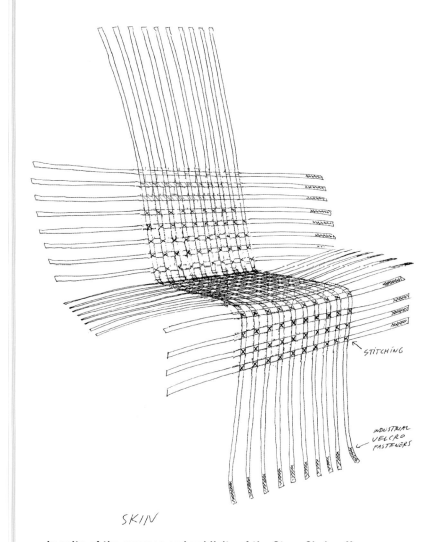

STITCHING

INDUSTRIAL VELCRO FASTENERS

SKIN

In spite of the success and publicity of the Strap Chair, offers from furniture manufacturers were not forthcoming. Evidently the strapping tape, with its "unfinished" character and the manual laboriousness of its application, was not a feasible material for any serious serial production. To continue the experiment, Boym Studio undertook a difficult attempt to translate the idea of the chair into the language of contract furniture.

We changed the frame to tubular aluminum to make it even
more lightweight. The web proved to be a harder challenge.
It needed to retain its airy, three-dimensional character, but
give up the manual weaving of individual straps. After much
trial and error, we constructed a prestitched net of cotton
webbing that was secured on the aluminum frame with
industrial Velcro fasteners. The resulting lounge chair, light
and comfortable, still sits in our studio. As of this writing,
there were no takers.

RE-DECORATION

In the beginning of 2001, decoration seemed like a timely topic to address. "At the outset of a new century, Minimalism appears to be strangely out of place. The economy, technology, culture, and fashion all seem to have reached the boiling point. This time of high tide asks for a new design attitude: more intense, more inclusive, and a bit more fun," we argued in the call for a show.

In an attempt to signal a new direction we decided to assemble a small group of New York designers who all agreed to contribute new works on the subject of decoration. While the exhibition fell short of starting a new movement, the opening events in May 2001 were certainly memorable. In order to transform an impersonal space in little time and with minimal expense, we covered the entire floor with thick layers of confetti. A visual manifestation of decoration itself, the confetti also provided an instant party spirit.

Taxicab chair—one of our own contributions for the exhibition—took inspiration from beaded seat covers favored by taxicab and van drivers. Instead of being placed on a chair, our seat cover *became* a chair. Oversized wooden balls played the role of functional decoration. Not surprisingly, the chair was comfortable and pleasant to sit on.

Seat cover in a van,
New York City

While we left one chair in clear wood with its subtle natural variations, the decorative quality of another was brought to the extreme. There, wooden balls were painted in fifteen different colors and assembled at random, without any prior sketch or layout. This "chaos theory" was supposed to guarantee decoration of a more complex order. Jordan Kovin, our assistant, took the task of randomness quite seriously, literally closing his eyes when reaching for the next ball during assembly. The completed chair left an indelible impression on many visitors to the exhibition. Unfortunately, making the Taxicab chairs proved too laborious for even a limited production.

SALVATION

In our disposable society, the life span of most objects is short. Anyone who ever walked into a thrift shop has seen, for example, shelves full of mismatched plates and cups, doomed to eternal oblivion and neglect. For years, we looked at these humble objects with pity, trying to think of their possible salvation, imagining ways to give them a new life. From dusty storage bins they would ascend to sparkling vitrines of galleries and exclusive design shops. But how?

We picked up some ceramic pieces and tried to assemble them into large and sumptuous compositions: vases, fruit bowls, table centerpieces. Originally, we attempted to fuse them together in a kiln with the help of a friend, a ceramic artist. This proved impossible, because mixed ceramics with different coefficients of expansion cracked in the process. For a while, it looked like the project was doomed. Then we read about Extreme Adhesive System, a high-tech glue made for the medical industry, which guaranteed a dishwasher-proof connection. Overcoming our initial reservations about gluing—a designer's taboo—we went ahead with new experiments.

Like any good game, the project had a few rules. Each porcelain component could not cost us more than three dollars. We assembled a few hundred pieces on a large table at our studio, and started our day with an hour of improvised object-making. In the evening, we glued the more successful compositions together for an overnight curing. Inevitably, each object was a one-of-a-kind piece. The new pieces celebrated the beauty of everyday objects in their infinite variations, a recurrent theme of our studio's work. In several weeks' time, over fifty objects were ready for an exhibition.

Discarded and neglected, ceramics in the basement of a thrift shop ask for salvation

"Like many designers, Constantin and Laurene Boym find inspiration and materials in all kinds of places, but for their most recent project they went to new depths: the basement of a thrift shop."
—Jeff Goldfarb, I.D. Magazine

At the exhibition, we suspended some vases in the air to demonstrate that they were fused together and not simply stacked. An Eames chase is in the background.

A proper context for a Salvation exhibition required an upscale location with a certain design panache. We were grateful to the furniture company Vitra USA for offering us the space of their New York showroom. Surrounded by timeless furniture classics, our compositions of plates and mugs suddenly exuded an aura of "design objects." To complete the impression, their price tag needed to be appropriately high. Murray Moss, the owner of a famed design store in Soho, suggested to ask for a Salvation vase "as much as people would pay for a real Wedgwood one." To our surprise, people happily acquiesced, and many pieces were sold at or shortly after the show.

On the first day of the year 2002, we received an e-mail from Marcel Wanders, a design colleague who had started his own production company in Amsterdam several months earlier. His company Moooi (standing for "beautiful" in Dutch, with an extra "o" for extra beauty) initiated a product line Moooi Weer, or "beautiful again," aimed at finding a new life for existing designs and objects.

"Following the rules of serendipity, we were working on a project 'together' some time ago," wrote Wanders. "You have made a project with second-hand ceramics as I did myself at the same moment. I was happy and not really surprised when I found out our mutual activities, our thinking having crossed before. I came up with the following idea, which I present to you as a proposal for the continuation for the project." Marcel Wanders asked us to produce a set of design guidelines for selecting and stacking the found objects. With instructions in hand, he continued, "We will find a stylist in Holland who will search for the plates, cups, and so on to build your pieces." Ingeniously, Wanders found a way to combine the idea of serial production with an infinite variety of individually found objects. From an artistic experiment, our project turned into a design product.

Moooi intends to produce no more than one hundred Salvation objects a year. The first fifteen pieces, skillfully made by stylist Rebecca Wijsbeek according to our instructions, were shown at the Furniture Fair in Milan in April 2002 to critical and commercial acclaim. "Perhaps we should take pictures of each one we make to start a collection," commented Wanders as the objects began to sell out.

1 bowl with pattern inside
ø 17cm

+

1 small white plate
ø 20cm

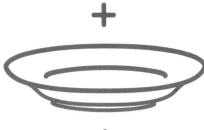

+

1 vase
solid colored
h: 13cm

+

1 American mug
solid colored (same color as vase)
h: 7.5cm
upside down

+

1 white saucer or small plate
ø 15cm
upside down

Memories of upstate
Top to bottom: High Falls, NY;
Kippelbush, NY; Pataukunk, NY
Facing page: Kerhonkson, NY

UPSTATE

In 1995, looking for a summer escape from the heat and energy of the city, we purchased a small country house in upstate New York. A mere two-hour drive from Manhattan, this region was known for its history and natural scenery, notwithstanding the economic stagnation of more recent decades. Driving along the country roads, I often thought about finding a way to commemorate the area and its understated and very American beauty.

Everyone is familiar with commercial souvenir plates featuring stereotypical views of European capitals or other picturesque tourist attractions. Instead, we envisioned a series of plates devoted to unknown, completely nondescript places in upstate New York. The views, which I took with a digital camera, were "almost all right," to use an expression of Robert Venturi. Yet there was always something slightly off-key about them, either a jumble of telephone wires overhead or a "wrong" car on the road.

The production of decals for picture plates usually requires very large quantities, which would rule out the feasibility of an experimental project like ours. But in 2002 we found a small company in Illinois with a new imaging technology, a high-resolution digital decal printer that made limited editions possible. Curiously, even though the project became a reality through high-tech digital advances, the technology itself was completely invisible in the final product, which retained an almost anonymous look. Even before the set of six plates was released, several American museums, including the Walker Art Center in Minneapolis, requested the plates for their upcoming exhibitions.

DESIGN SOUVENIRS

In 1994, as the Cooper-Hewitt Museum in New York was preparing to celebrate its centennial, it received a title of the National Design Museum. As a member of the museum's Design Advisory Committee, I was attending monthly meetings where the imminent celebrations were planned in great detail. One of the issues that came up regularly was the need for new kinds of souvenirs and gift items for the museum's shop and for giveaways. Inevitably, I started to experiment with this "assignment."

Museum souvenirs traditionally are limited to mostly decorative things. For a design museum, however, it was essential to emphasize that design is a part of everyone's daily life. We selected a number of conventional, ready-made objects for their iconic value. The museum's new logo by Drenttel Doyle (which fortunately had a graphic emphasis on the word "design") was supposed to be imprinted directly on their surfaces. While the objects still remain useful, they also acquire a certain design aura, enabling people to look at them with inordinate attention.

A completed proposal of new souvenirs was submitted to the museum, where it received a lukewarm reaction, was deemed "uncommercial," and shelved.

FOR CULTURE'S SAKE

A strange incident took place in the city of Seoul on September 2, 1994. Dozens of angry South Korean students attacked an exhibition of traditional Japanese ceramics at a prestigious museum, smashing display cases and destroying valuable artifacts. The protesters were demonstrating not against Japan's arts and crafts but against the Japanese government's past policies toward Korea. So why did they take on a cultural institution to express their anger?

Their choice would probably not surprise some of today's leading political scientists. According to Samuel P. Huntington, a professor of government at Harvard, the great boundaries that used to divide humankind are no longer primarily ideological or economic—they are cultural. Throughout most of the twentieth century, conflicts between communism, fascism, and Western liberal democracy formed the basis for human history. The confrontation between communism and democracy, for example, drew boundaries across almost all continents, with the Berlin Wall its most visible manifestation.

But with the end of the Cold War, the globe can no longer be separated into first, second, and third worlds. It is more meaningful now to group countries in terms of their shared heritage of language, customs, and values. "The Velvet Curtain of culture has replaced the Iron Curtain of ideology in Europe," attests Huntington. Indeed, contemporary developments on either side of Europe illustrate in different ways the validity of culture as a political concept. In the West, the leaders of the European Union invoke a homogenized culture as they pursue the abolition of borders and the establishment of a common currency. On the other hand, tragic events in the former Yugoslavia show how the elusive line of cultural difference could easily become a front line of bloody confrontation. As the world becomes a smaller place—people now move around the globe with great dexterity as refugees, laborers, entrepreneurs, students, and travelers—and interaction between many different peoples increases, these closer contacts can intensify feelings of cultural identity.

Moreover, in our "soft" postindustrial economy, culture provides the backbone to strategic economic development. Most developed countries have already witnessed an economic shift from production-based manufacturing to knowledge-based industries like software, telecommunications, entertainment, and tourism. Culture is soon expected to become the world's largest industry. In the last decade of the twentieth century, American cultural exports, such as popular movies, music, and information, constituted a large part of our economical well-being. From theme parks to museum stores, there is a market direction to meet a worldwide public demand for culture-related merchandise.

One could argue that design as a discipline is supposed to relate to the world at large. And if the world is changing, so

Souvenirs in Brussels and New York—at the beginning of the twenty-first century, with rapid growth of tourism and travel, proliferation of culture-related artifacts has reached new heights.

"The past must be preserved and celebrated in full-scale authentic copy; a philosophy of immortality as duplication." —Umberto Eco, Travels Into Hyperreality

Souvenir collections of Russian immigrants in Washington, D.C. and Brookline, Massachusetts

"Their rooms filled with diasporic souvenirs are not altars to their unhappiness, but rather places for communication and conversation. They do not manage to live in the eternal present of the American myth, but neither can they afford to dwell in the past."
—Svetlana Boym, The Future of Nostalgia

should design. Since the spread of the Industrial Revolution, design has internalized the century's reigning economic, technological, and social influences. The entire vocabulary of the design language reflects this: We talk about practicality, cost-effectiveness, new materials and manufacturing processes, and human benefit. Good design is often synonymous with design that "works." Nonfunctional objects, on the contrary, are automatically banished from the field. Such a view, however, may no longer be adequate. In a new world where culture has become a major determinant, design will have to find a new paradigm, a different mode of "working"—one based less on performance and more on communication, emotion, and joy.

In this respect, it is worthwhile to look at souvenirs. These objects represent an important part of our civilization's material culture. They can be found in every home, regardless of a person's economic or social status, and they can be as different as a miniature marble leaning Tower of Pisa and a monkey made of coconuts. Not surprisingly, the sale of souvenirs amounts to big business—more than $20 billion annually in the United States alone. Yet the entire phenomenon of the souvenir is largely excluded from the high culture of design and completely ignored by most design professions. If we accept that design is a way of communicating ideas, then souvenirs are quintessential design objects. They can carry complex layers of information, from "programmed" messages to personal sentiments.

Beverly Gordon, a professor of environmental studies at the University of Wisconsin, makes a distinction between souvenirs and mementos: The former are commercially produced, universally recognized, purchased objects; the latter are individually saved or found objects that have a deeply personal meaning. It is the first category that provides an interesting case study for product designers. A souvenir is manufactured to serve as a reminder (the word, in French, means "to remember") of a non-ordinary experience, place, or culture. The object works metonymically, as a part or a fragment that evokes larger places and events. Its partialness, however, is always supplemented by a personal narrative or recollection.
The popular appeal of souvenirs is rooted precisely in this combination of material object and immaterial, fleeting sentiment. Unlike many "serious" products or appliances, the souvenir always contains a built-in emotional value, such as a memory of a past journey or the affection of a faraway friend. Preservation of memory serves as profound motivation for a lifetime passion of collecting.

Once in New York, I visited the apartment of two elderly Holocaust survivors. They met in Europe shortly after the Liberation, and soon got married, but could not conceive a child, her health being seriously damaged after years in the camp. One day, the man gave his wife a small toy bear, a touching souvenir of the family they were never to have. Collecting and giving each other bears has become their lifelong tradition. Eventually, their spacious apartment became home to over a thousand bears of every conceivable material,

Bears of survival: a collection in a New York City apartment

size, and look. These are not functional useful objects, and most of them have little or no "artistic value." Yet how is it possible not to take this collection seriously, not to treat it with proper affection and respect?

People's attitudes toward souvenirs, though, can best be described as a love-hate relationship. Everyone has and buys them, but they are easily dismissed and thrown away. Designers are the most critical, instantly relegating these keepsakes as kitsch—but you can always find them in designers' own homes. Often, they try to find the tackiest, most outlandish souvenir possible to bring home for the amusement of their peers. Why is it that a certain silliness and tastelessness prevails—and is even appreciated—in this product genre? According to Beverly Gordon, such objects help to accomplish an "inversion of the ordinary"—just as when fun and recreation briefly substitute for the realities of everyday life. When on vacation, people tend to go to the extremes of good taste, spending money on strange, whimsical, nonfunctional items precisely because they would not do it in their daily existence. In this sense, a souvenir's emotional, accessible, funny design is essential for it to function properly. "Inversion of the ordinary" puts souvenirs in opposition to objects of "good" design, with their characteristic usefulness, seriousness, and value. Instead, souvenirs offer the option of different attitudes and aesthetics—for people who are, at least temporarily, not practical, serious, or thrifty.

Traditionally, souvenirs have been manufactured exclusively for the tourist market. But in a new, shrinking world—as the

Cultural ID: souvenirs in a taxicab and in a shop window, New York City, 2001

mobility of the population exponentially increases—souvenirs, in a different form, are among the few objects from home that can accompany a person to a foreign land. Souvenirs, then, have the potential of being transformed from a superfluous product of consumption to an object of emotional survival. Instead of a tourist cliché, a souvenir can serve as a proud representation of a person's cultural identity. Think of all those souvenirs that multinational New York City taxicab drivers display on the dashboards of their cars. In the aftermath of the September 11 events, many owners of New York shops placed American flags and souvenirs next to symbols of their own cultures as a message of peace and understanding.

In a world divided along the lines of culture, such object-symbols can no longer be marginalized. Almost always, souvenirs are designed anonymously—no well-known designer, it seems, would ever attach his or her name to one. And designing a new souvenir is rarely given as an assignment in design schools. So there has been little progress in the genre; all the design movements of the past few decades have just passed it by. But, hopefully, these attitudes will change. The world needs a lot of new souvenirs—for culture's sake.

A version of this article originally appeared in **Metropolis** *magazine in November 1995. Reprinted with permission.*

One of the most unusual seminars of souvenir design took place at Bauhaus University in Weimar, Germany in 1999. To celebrate that year's designation of Weimar as the cultural capital of Europe, students (under the direction of Axel Kufus, Kuno Prey, Stefan Schiefer, and others) created a series of souvenirs devoted to Weimar's famous citizens. The objects were produced in a limited edition. From the top: J. W. Goethe rubber pacifier (by Harald Kollwitz); Goethe-Schiller Monument wooden toy (by Petra Polking)

The idea for Missing Monuments originated with this building. Although never built, the 1200-foot-high Palace of the Soviets (Boris Iofan and others, 1931–1956) was regarded as the most important structure of the Soviet Union. For over twenty years, the designs for the palace had figured prominently in Moscow city plans and guidebooks, as if the building actually existed.

MISSING MONUMENTS

It is not surprising that our longtime fascination with souvenirs has culminated in a desire to design some of our own. The challenge, as we saw it, was to look at this familiar product type in an unfamiliar way and to propose objects that would retain all the usual souvenir appeal but also have new meaning.

The Missing Monuments project dealt with a small part of the large souvenir world: the typology of miniature buildings. These ubiquitous objects (think of Empire State Buildings or Eiffel Towers of every conceivable size) have been much ridiculed, yet they make up many cherished private collections. Our souvenirs were different in one fundamental respect: they were replicas of famous buildings that did not exist. These structures may have been destroyed, or they may have never even been built, such as visionary architecture that often exerts a profound cultural influence. When a souvenir's referent does not exist, a small replica assumes a new and different meaning. The object becomes an indispensable thing, the only material manifestation left of a memory or idea. And, of course, these items make unique collectibles.

The appeal of miniature buildings goes beyond private collections. Models of buildings appear in medieval cathedrals, usually held by a saint in a gesture of heavenly protection. Perhaps for similar reasons, miniature monuments often serve as ceremonial gifts presented by government delegations on their official trips abroad.

A first set of prototypes for Missing Monuments was made in 1995. The following year, Arlene Hirst of *Metropolitan Home* published a half-page article on them in her magazine. Suddenly, the telephone began to ring. After several hundred phone inquiries, it became clear that we had to somehow organize the production of these objects. The permanence and weight of Missing Monuments seemed essential, hence cast bronze was originally considered as an appropriate "monumental" material. The cost of lost-wax casting ruled this option out. Instead, we produced the buildings in bonded bronze (a composite material that combines finely ground metal powder with a bonding resin). The miniatures appeared heavy and solid, as if made of metal, yet it was possible to cast them in inexpensive rubber molds. Soon we found ourselves in the mail-order souvenir business.

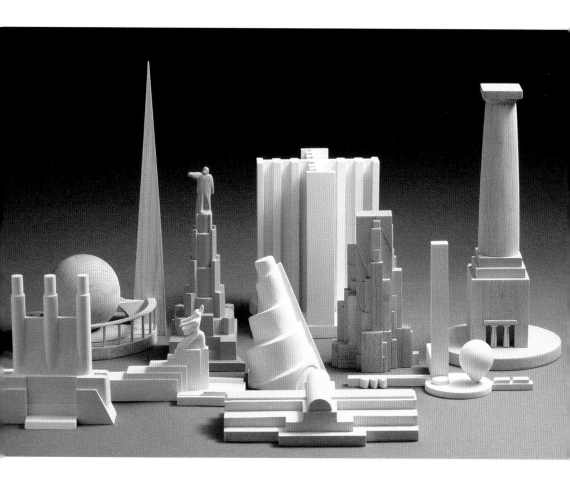

1. Ivan Leonidov, Ministry of Heavy Industry, Moscow, 1934

2. Solomon's Temple, Jerusalem, 950 B.C.

3. McKim, Mead & White, Pennsylvania Station, New York, 1904–1910

4. Abbey Church of Cluny, France, 1088–1130

5. Aldo Rossi, Teatro Del Mondo, Venice, 1979

6. Leonardo da Vinci, Church of Central Plan, Italy, 1490s

7. Erich Mendelson, Factory for Optical Instruments, Germany, 1914

8. Antonio Sant'Elia, Power Station, Italy, 1913

9. Pharos, Alexandria, 332 B.C.

10. Boris Iofan, Palace of the Soviets, Moscow, 1932–56

11. Etienne-Louis Boullée, Newton's Cenotaph, France, 1784

12. Temple of Artemis, Ephesus, 340 B.C.

13. Mausoleum, Halicarnassus, 353 B.C.

14. Vladimir Tatlin, Monument to the Third International, Russia, 1919

15. Adolf Loos, Chicago Tribune Column, Chicago, 1922

16. Ernest Flagg, Singer Tower, New York, 1908

17. Joseph Paxton, Crystal Palace, London, 1851

18. Ziggurat, Ur (Mesopotamia), 2100 B.C.

19. Claude-Nicolas Ledoux, Cannon Foundry, Chaux, 1773–79

1

The first edition of Missing Monuments included ten buildings; more were added each year. An entire alternative architectural history could be seen through the prism of these small objects: from the ruined Seven Wonders of the World, to the utopian projects of the Russian avant-garde, to the lost pavilions of the World's Fairs. A short description of the building and of the reasons why it was chosen to be in the edition was included in every box.

8

9

10

14

15

16

2

3

4

5

6

7

11

12

13

17

18

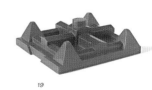

19

In 1996 I received an invitation to take part in an exhibition at
the Russian pavilion of the Sixth International Biennial of
Architecture in Venice. Yuri Avvakumov, an old Moscow
colleague and the curator of the pavilion, envisioned a theme
very much in sync with the Missing Monuments project. The
installation, called A Depository of Russian Utopia, featured a
mountain-like archive of flat files. In each drawer a single sheet
of an unrealized architectural project was placed for display
and study.

The hall next to the archive was left empty but for the whirlwind
of Missing Monuments. Over three hundred tiny objects were
mounted directly on the walls, casting long oblique shadows.
For this installation, we produced a special edition of
miniatures in translucent resin of nostalgic pastel colors.
We provided a pedestal in the middle of the space as a shop
counter—after all, these miniatures were souvenirs intended for
sale. All of the stock was sold out during the opening, mobbed
by hundreds of guests. For three remaining months, the empty
counter stood as an empty token of a missed business
opportunity.

Since the beginning of the Missing Monuments project, I had a dream of constructing them at a scale larger than four to five inches high. A chance came in 2001, when the Parrish Art Museum in Southampton invited us to submit a project for their show of contemporary garden follies. Missing Monuments looked like an ideal choice for the theme. The introspective, contemplative, or melancholy spirit often evoked by traditional garden follies is inherent in the imagery of a missing building.

The follies, proposed for the grounds of exclusive Hamptons estates, were planned to be approximately eight feet in height, with their materials and construction methods determined by the nature of the original building. In the accompanying text we wrote, "Boym Studio is willing to supply construction drawings and specifications of these and other Missing Monuments follies upon special request." The rendering sold at auction, but no building offers followed.

Pedestal of a monument that was destroyed in 1991 on Lubyanka Square in Moscow

MONUMENTAL PROPAGANDA

In 1993, Russian-American conceptual artists Komar & Melamid issued a call asking the world's artistic community for advice on what to do with monumental propaganda in the former Soviet Union. The topic had a certain urgency. Hundreds of statues, devoid of any meaning or purpose, remained standing in the ex-Soviet cities. Some had already been demolished. The project generated over one hundred responses, which formed a traveling exhibition.

While many participants submitted cartoons or ironic artistic commentaries, we envisioned a practical pragmatic proposal. We proposed to turn monumental propaganda into "monumental advertising" by leasing various Lenin statues to Western corporations for a fee, payable to the cash-strapped Russian cities. In a startling transformation, the monuments would now signify the ultimate victory of capitalism. At the same time, the statues would remain intact in their key urban sites, thus preserving the cities' contexts.

The Nike Lenin Monument became one of the most publicized images from the exhibition. Unfortunately, the complexities of the political situation in Russia prevented this or any other submitted project from being realized, even on a temporary basis.

"It arrived in the mail with the
Christmas catalogues, slipped
inside a bright red, zippered
plastic bag. But it wasn't very
cheery reading."
—Jura Koncius, Washington
Post

SOUVENIRS
FOR THE
END OF THE
CENTURY

In 1997 the idea of the forthcoming millennium seemed fresh
and exciting. We felt that marking the event with an edition
of special millennium souvenirs was an appropriate creative
contribution. This was the beginning of a three-year-long
project, a mail-order catalog Souvenirs for the End of the
Century. "While we no longer expect the world to come to
an end, we all still share a particular mood of introspection,
a desire to look back and to draw comparisons, and a sense
of closure and faint hope. Above all, the end of the century
is about memory," began the first edition of the catalog.
We planned to reissue the catalog for three years and to
stop production after the century's official end on December
31, 2000. The edition of every souvenir was thus to be limited,
and we intended to consecutively number all pieces. The high
prices of most items were quite intentional, as we wanted
people to keep and care for their souvenirs for a very long time.

We sent out the first edition in November 1998. The spread
of the mailing list was facilitated by nonstop press and media
coverage, often ironic and not very flattering. Yet even sarcastic
reviews always brought more orders.

right: Fathers of Modern Art:
Mies van der Rohe

facing page: Bill Clinton's
Stirring Spoons
top to bottom: Stock Market,
Sex Scandal, Healthcare Bill

Fathers of Modern Art was a collection of miniature sculptural busts made of bonded marble. Portraits of these high priests of modernism in art, architecture, and culture looked amusingly displaced in the populist format of little busts.

Meredith Beau, a designer from Little Rock, Arkansas, collaborated with us on a series of souvenir silver spoons devoted to the presidency of her famous fellow citizen, Bill Clinton, the last American president of the twentieth century. Not surprisingly, the most popular of the spoons proved to be the Sex Scandal, with its handle modeled after an open zipper. Originally, we planned many more collaborative projects for the catalog, but this idea proved too challenging to follow through.

Souvenirs of tragedies, top to bottom: sand from the Bay of Pigs (Cuba); plaque of the Nuclear Missile Crisis (USA); piece of the Berlin Wall (Germany)

BUILDINGS OF DISASTER

The most controversial—and the most successful—line of the catalog was a collection called Buildings of Disaster. These monuments enter the collective memory when tragic or terrible events take place inside or around their walls. Some of these buildings may have been prized architectural landmarks—others, nondescript anonymous structures. But disaster changes everything. The images of burning or exploded buildings make a different, populist history of architecture, one based on emotional involvement rather than on scholarly appreciation. People's attraction to the disaster sites goes beyond the tabloid and television frenzy. Inevitably, the tragic sites become involuntary monuments and tourist destinations.

While a notion of souvenirs devoted to tragedy may appear shocking, it is actually based on a long history of precedents. The first known "souvenirs" were brought back by the Crusaders from their voyages to the Holy Land. These included pieces of the Cross and the stones from the Golgotha, which were fabricated on site by enterprising merchants. During the French Revolution of 1789, small wooden models of the guillotine were sold throughout Europe, where they briefly became a fad. (Reportedly, Goethe criticized them as bad taste.) Today, one can buy small pieces of the Berlin Wall on eBay. Buildings of Disaster continues this souvenir category at a special and uncertain moment of our human history.

The starting point for the project came in the aftermath of the Oklahoma City bombing, when the ruined silhouette of the Alfred P. Murrah Federal Building instantly became one of the world's most recognizable icons. The miniatures that followed addressed American history (Texas School Book Depository), environmental disaster (Chernobyl, Three Mile Island), and political and government scandal (the Watergate, the Waco, Texas ranch). The World Trade Center was also featured as the site of the 1993 bombing. The most popular building in the collection was the Unabomber's Cabin—an archetypal image of the little American house that turned sinister upon closer inspection.

The information for making the miniatures came from the pages of newspapers and magazines. From the beginning, we decided not to get too archival, but rather operate with what had already been sifted through media representations. It felt important not to get into architectural details, but to allow for generalizations and even distortions to heighten the emotional impact of the object. The buildings' material, bonded nickel, added to the drama with its weight and feel of solid metal.

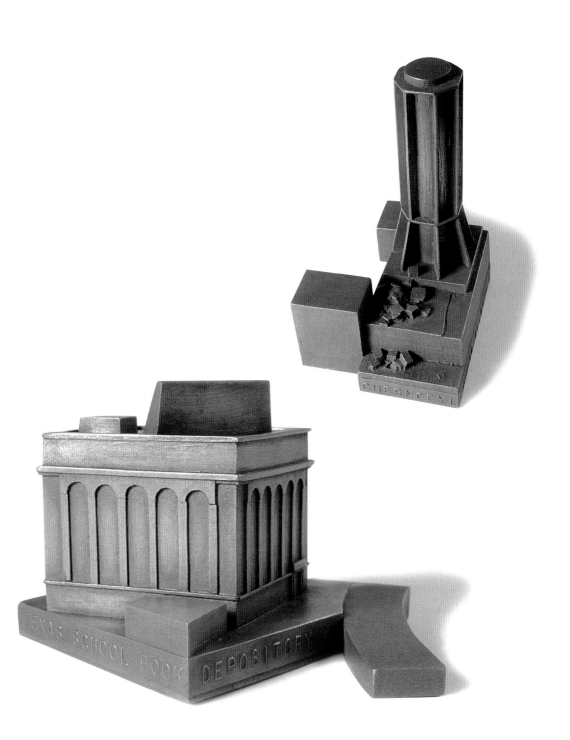

Souvenirs often incorporate additional functions to appear more useful. Our buildings define usefulness in different terms.

In 1999 Murray Moss, the owner of a celebrated design store in SoHo, made us a surprising offer to carry the Buildings of Disaster among the twentieth-century design classics in his shop. For Moss, the models are "honest objects. Here is something that is not unabashedly hiding behind another function. They give you a tangible place to put your feelings." At the Moss store, the buildings have become a best-selling item, and they continue to sell as of this writing.

Many people who liked Buildings of Disaster have considered them strange and eccentric artworks. For us, they were objects of design, not art. Their distribution channel was a mail-order catalog, and their price ($95 apiece), while not exactly cheap, was certainly not a typical price for art.

In the 1990s, culture and information became American largest exports, both in terms of dollars and of global influence. The new information-based economy requires new generations of products with a different mode of "working"—one based less on performance and more on communication, emotion, and desire. I have described this new mode as "fuzzy function." It is fuzzy because a product's purpose is not immediately clear—it fulfills an immaterial need. Such a product aims to become an object of desire, an instant collectible and keepsake—thus avoiding the vicious circle of obsolescence and disposability.

In March 2000, Herbert Muschamp published a full-page article, "The Dionysian Drama of Today's Design," in the *New York Times*. It was largely devoted to Buildings of Disaster. "Design has abandoned Socrates for Nietzsche," wrote Muschamp. For him, the last century's design had largely operated on a rational, Apollinian basis. The new design of the new century would appeal to emotion, as if in a Dionysian revel. "The operating logic here is intuitive rather than analytic." Our miniatures were cited as a notable example of new designs that "deal explicitly with the tragic dimension."

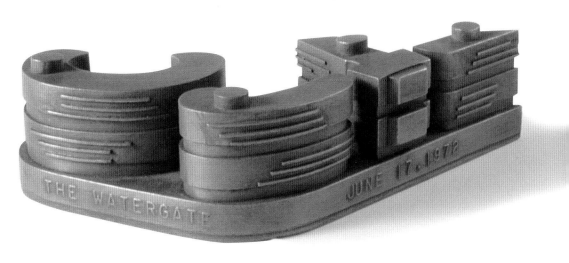

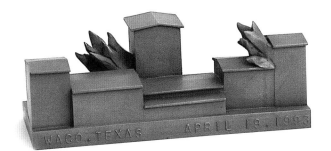

"The monuments are EX-quisite...more beautiful than I imagined. I unpacked them last night after an especially bad day and they totally lifted my spirits."
—Lisa Stone, Chicago

"I'm an enthusiast of your 'Souvenirs for the End of the Century.' I collected a group at a local retail store, and now have doubled my collection, with this latest box from you. These are a fantastic way to 'experience' some very remarkable architecture and history."
—D. Ostrow, Los Angeles

Buildings of Disaster at the First International Design Biennial in Saint-Etienne, France

"When we visit the Eiffel Tower we can leave with a keepsake, a golden Eiffel Tower in a snowball. When we turn the TV off, no snowball from Chernobyl will decorate the fireplace. Nothing to remember the images of the catastrophe, the dead. It's this emptiness that Constantin Boym wants to fill with his small objects."
—Pascal Yanou

In the summer of 2000 alone, the Buildings of Disaster were on display in three New York museums simultaneously: at the Whitney Museum of American Art, at the Cooper-Hewitt National Design Museum, and at the American Craft Museum. San Francisco MoMA has acquired them for its permanent design collection. The objects were featured in over one hundred publications worldwide; they have appeared on CNN, ABC, and the Metro Channel.

Our best recognition, however, came from our direct customers, many of whom have become regular correspondents. Among the owners of Buildings of Disaster are directors John Waters, the Coen brothers, Tracy Ullman, and Woody Allen; actor Kevin Spacey; producer Joel Silver; and architects Philip Johnson, Stanley Tigerman, and Alex Gorlin. One of the most unusual requests came from a retiring FBI officer who had actually arrested the Unabomber back in 1997. Many customers called to suggest their own ideas for a building. As the result of one such grass-roots campaign, we added a miniature commemorating the O. J. Car Chase to the collection in 2000, even though it was not, strictly speaking, a building.

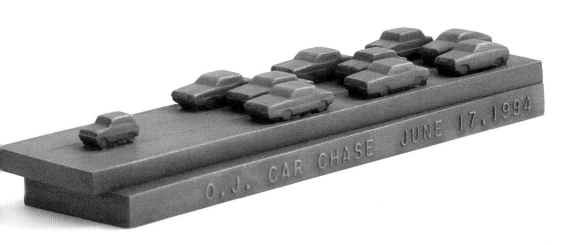

Rosie the Riveter: Laurene inspects the buildings ready for shipment.

By the fall of 2001 the catalog was practically over. As per our early promise we had stopped the buildings' production and were selling off the remainders.

Then September 11 came. Having witnessed the collapse of the north tower, I stumbled into our studio. One of the first phone calls I received that morning was an inquiry about the World Trade Center souvenir. I hung up in dismay. Many more phone calls with similar questions came that day. The turning point came the next morning when I got an e-mail request from a person whose office had perished in one of the towers. How was it possible to say no? Obviously, there was a real emotional need for the souvenir, a need that had to be fulfilled. That day, we decided to reissue the World Trade Center miniature as a fund-raising effort and to donate the proceeds to the September 11 Fund. Linda Hales of the *Washington Post* published a small but inspiring article, "New Poignancy for a Tragic Memento," and an avalanche of orders came along.

Small models of the World Trade Center, often made by children, formed part of many makeshift memorials in New York City.

In November 2001, the project continued with the September 11 Memorial Set, which included a new miniature of the World Trade Center and one of the Pentagon.

Along with a sudden and unexpected transformation of our position—from a provocative design comment into a fund-raising patriotic effort—the essence of the project had changed as well. In the fall of 2001, it was no longer possible for a New Yorker to be an outside commentator. We had been thrown into the middle of the events. Inevitably, some controversy was generated, both on the grounds of taste and of capitalizing on disaster. Yet letters to our studio confirmed an overwhelming need for a mnemonic device, an object where people could put their feelings and make their memory permanent. "We have turned to your Buildings of Disaster as a way to deal with this tragedy and will share them with students in the coming days and weeks," wrote Lisa Stone, a curator from Chicago. How could souvenirs possibly be of help? The answer is far from clear. People put their own meaning into the miniatures, and they find their own personal ways to use them as material for memories or memorials.

TEN THOUGHTS ON TWO PEOPLE IN ONE STUDIO
Steven Skov Holt

ONE. Constantin Boym and his wife and partner Laurene Leon Boym are "curious Boyms" in their own right. I intend this as a compliment of the highest order. They have taken the uncommon currency of curiosity and made it their own. In so doing, they have released a fascinating array of product and environmental projects. But even more significantly, they have invested in curiosity as a way to fashion an alternative model for what a design firm can be. At this point in time, this is an important virtue. The American design profession, and more generally our cultural milieu, has veered sharply toward the widespread acceptance of corporate values. Experimental possibilities no longer have to be shot down or shut down by outside forces. Today, they are often eliminated by the very artists and designers who would otherwise produce them. Boym Studio has shown that it is possible to be a commercially viable company yet be simultaneously engaged in a radical, trans-historical critique of American material culture.

TWO. Perhaps only someone who is an outsider, someone who by definition is from beyond the boundaries of the familiar, can see American contemporary culture with the combination of clarity and amazement that it truly deserves. If so, Constantin may be the ideal guide. A Moscow-trained architect who shifted to the architecture of objects while getting a graduate degree at Domus Academy in Milan, he sees American myths, rituals, and propaganda for what they are—as social constructs, no better and no worse than any other society's. When Boym's talents combine with Laurene's graduate degree in industrial design from Pratt Institute, and her insider knowledge of American culture along with her ersatz sensibility for what is hip and trend-worthy, they are able to synthesize a unique vision of who they are relative to virtually everyone else in the design profession. In this sense, Boym Studio practices design in the way that Jean Baudrillard, Andrei Codrescu, and Umberto Eco practice writing—by finding meaning and significance in the ordinary and already well trodden.

THREE. Constantin and Laurene's work is not simply curious but relentlessly so. A sense of deep engagement characterizes Boym Studio's *modus operandi.* Being relentlessly curious is their way of being, their natural state, their philosophical essence. It is the intellectual substrate of the interrogative process upon which their designs are built, the hallmark of every project that they do. Make no mistake: this is a radical design ethic, one not afraid of going where the truth of their investigations may lead them. Artist and designer Dan Friedman regularly spoke of his own radical project—a way of calling into question specific cultural elements of a design and, by so doing, getting directly to the root of things in a world that is ever more artificial and complex. Like Friedman's effort, Boym Studio's struggle is not only to create but to comprehend; to not only make fashionable objects, but to fashion meaning through the making of those very same objects. That is why both have had such a strong focus on the expression of personal, cultural, and domestic values at a time when corporations have overwhelmingly determined the flavor, texture, and characteristics of daily life. Revisit Boym Studio's edible dinnerware that premiered in *ID Magazine's* Fantasy Portfolio in 1987 and glimpse a fresh approach hard at work at improving upon one of civilization's oldest tools.

Edible plates, project for
ID Magazine in 1987 (designed
with Lev Zeitlin)

Top: Gummy Bear Chair,
competition project for A Chair
for Barbie, received an Honorable
Mention in 1996

Bottom: Less Is More, a shelf
for collectors, designed in 2000
and manufactured by Pure
Design in Canada

FOUR. The work of Boym Studio always emerges out of a cogent
but evolving philosophy. It has never been about merely serving
up an easily digestible style or offering the hungry consumer a
fast feast of visual calories. That is why, when taken as a whole,
the projects of Boym Studio do not make an immediate pattern.
This observation formed the basis of numerous conversations
I have had with Constantin over the years. Wouldn't it be easier,
we'd say, if we spent our time developing a style that we could
simply apply like a decal to whatever project came along? We
knew it had to be easier than what we were doing, and we
wondered what it would be like to command a seemingly more
emotionally spontaneous form language such as those of, say,
Philippe Starck. But we might as well have been talking about
getting gills to breath underwater, or fashioning a shirt pocket
that turned aluminum cans into platinum ingots. We were
already far too caught up in a way of designing that was
fundamentally intellectual; work began with an idea, not an
impulse. From the beginning, Boym Studio has been cognitively
predisposed toward an active, and often proactive, thinking role
for the designer; their process demands no less than the
difficult route.

FIVE. Boym Studio's philosophy—particularly visible in its
formative years from the mid-1980s to the early 1990s—was
based on a creative process that was equal parts inventive
reclamation and creative reformulation. I met Constantin before
I met Laurene, probably during the summer of 1986, and I soon
learned from him that he felt it was no longer possible to invent
anything truly new. At first, I found this daunting. But the more
we spoke, the more I saw that he always had a work-around,

an idea about how to positively counter whatever gloomy assessments we came up with about a specific design challenge—even his own. He may have grown up as a Russian acculturated to struggle and to wage the good fight, but along the way he also developed a sense of humor and began to embrace the famous can-do spirit of American optimism. It made for a compelling combination on both a human as well as a professional level. Even more, I believe it was this contradictory combination of qualities that allowed him to see the vast infinity of elements making up our past and our present as if they were an endless supply closet. Just as he showed in the later "Searstyle" project, he and Laurene were ready to review, reinterpret, and reassemble design from the floor on up. This, I felt, was a quietly heroic thing: the perpetual struggle against all odds of the human spirit to express and unfetter itself. In Constantin's actions, I saw a designer admitting that design—at least as everyone then knew it—was no longer the right question or the right answer. I saw a cultural innovator saying that innovation had to dramatically change because we were at the end of history, and if we wanted to truly face the crisis that design and late-stage capitalism presented at the end of the twentieth century, we had to accept the challenge of becoming more human by embracing our limitations, not running from them.

SIX. Through their design work, Boym Studio propagates the view that we live in an age of flux, not certainty. It is a moment when our images, objects, and spaces need to reflect the transformative tempo of the times rather than strive for eternal values. Ettore Sottsass, Jr., wrote in *Design Since 1945*, "My

Coffee Table Book Table from Searstyle collection, 1992.

Egg Handle, prototypes for The Pull of Beauty exhibition in New York, 1996

Floor Lamp and Candy Dish from the Recycle collection, 1988.

answer is always the same. If a society plans obsolescence, the only possible enduring design is one that deals with obsolescence, a design that comes to terms with it, maybe accelerating it, maybe confronting it, maybe ironizing [sic] it, maybe getting along with it. The only design that does not endure is the one that in such a society looks for metaphysics, looks for the absolute, for eternity." Constantin and Laurene believe that this is the only way that products can be true to themselves, to their materials, and to us. Through the reuse or "remanufacture" of what has already been produced, they posit that what is being sold now as an end product will in many instances become the raw material for a new generation of designers to come. We are no longer expecting a Robert Hughesian "shock of the new" in consumer design, but a Boymian "shock of the familiar" driven by a new class of products capable of physical if not psychological transformation. Why should the new generation of designers build an expensive virgin mold when they can get what they need off the shelves? This points out that there is no one perfect solution to any design problem; but, instead, there are a series of solutions, each of whose efficacy can be decided only on a case-by-case basis. Examples of Boym Studio's remanufactured work comprise everything from the used cans and bottles that form the basis of the Recycle series to the automobile antennas that were used in a mass-produced Antenna Clock for Morphos that riffed on George Nelson's iconic time pieces of the 1950s. Boym Studio's view of contemporary design practice is that it necessitates remanufacture and careful critique because this is the best and sometimes only way to hack the complexities of our cultural codes. If you thought the Human Genome

Project was immense, try hacking the multivalent and heterodox codes of American culture!

SEVEN. Nonetheless, this is the direction to which the best of Boym Studio's work points. This work asks questions about consumption, change, status, contemporary existence, and what the meaning of an "eco-designer" might be. Ironically, one possible definition of the new eco-designer may be provided by Constantin and Laurene themselves: that of individuals working together to question, juxtapose, and rearrange culturally familiar yet widely underappreciated elements of everyday life. The message from Boym Studio is that beauty is to be made, not discovered, and that creativity does not originate from the lone genius suffering in a garret but rather from a collaborative, hybridized, and impure process that is life affirming and worthy of celebration. Even as natural nature is disappearing, artificial nature—and the role and responsibility of design as represented by Boym Studio—is increasing exponentially.

EIGHT. Boym Studio has often left their work willfully open-ended. The Antenna Clock, for example, was not finished until the person putting it on their wall decided how far to extend each of the twelve antenna vanes. The Mona Lisa Clock only formed a complete portrait of La Gioconda at noon and midnight. The Chair Project was about imagining the most minimal skeletal form possible for a chair, and then envisioning its various accessories in a modular fashion so that a consumer could "plug and play" with any particular combination of styles, periods, or motifs that they found stimulating. On top of these, Boym Studio's projects tend to allow the consumer to change

Peg Chair, structural frame and custom variations, model, 1990–93 (designed with Steven Skov Holt)

their design with minor cost and effort. This is another radical notion: the idea that a designer would give up a say in the final form that a design takes—and would let the lay consumer [gasp!] decide for themselves! This is what I believe true postindustrial design will be about: the democratization of the creative act.

NINE. There is a more disturbing trend at work, however. Boym Studio embodies one of the more rigorous and material culture-based approaches to the process and production of design today. Yet as mid-career professionals, Constantin and Laurene still have not found even a single truly magical client that can afford them the opportunity to take their work to the next level. As a colleague interested in expanding the possibilities for what design can be, I am dismayed that Boym Studio's phone does not ring off the hook and that their mailbox is not jam-packed with RFPs (requests for proposals). I have come to believe that their intelligence is misunderstood by most in the business community. I imagine Boym Studio is seen as a "wild card" and potential chaos-creator by the MBAs and executives who govern any particular project. So instead of corporations getting what they really need—innovative thinking, deep curiosity, and radical creativity at every level of the project—they get what they probably deserve—a me-too, yes-sir, and inherently more conservative and nonthreatening design partner.

TEN. From the very beginning, Boym Studio has brought the realm of contemporary art-making into the design profession. While their target has occasionally been that of a mass demographic, their norm has been to focus—like Andrea Branzi, Constantin's mentor at Domus Academy—on what may

Conversation Piece, a sketch for an ashtray, c.1996

be called "limited semantic groups." This focus on visual culture-aware niche markets has allowed Boym Studio to employ some of the strategies of art-making in their design work. They have used these strategies to veer far away from the type of neutralized, lowest-common-denominator design that is often said to have the best shot at global acceptance. Instead, Boym Studio has created products that seek out their own constituency. By remaining true to these loyal microcultures, Boym Studio has established itself as the real deal. Even when Constantin was by himself in the mid-1980s, that edge was apparent. He first lived in Manhattan in a downtown rental just off Houston Street. But it was no ordinary residence. It was a home—and a studio—that was the urban equivalent of a tool shed with running water and electricity. That place, the smallest of all of my friend's spaces, became the unofficial clubhouse for parties disguised as meetings, sexual escapades disguised as love, and even occasionally the reverse of both. I will always remember Constantin living there during the summer of 1988 when it was unrelentingly hot for weeks. Every few hours, he would head to the store to buy cold watermelon—a crude and only semieffective way to keep cool. As his colleagues, we were horrified for him. He seemed delirious half the time or more. But in the eventual coolness of those summer evenings, he repeatedly assured us over chilled vodka and beer that this was the *best* place he had ever lived. With that perspective, I knew his success was all but assured. Given that beginning, is it any wonder that he and Laurene are now able to create products that bear the attributes of a gift, and that these products are possessive of an almost lapidary literary presence?

Constantin and Laurene in search of inspiration at Home Depot, c.1995

PRODUCTS

Products for
ELIKA

We met our first design client at a trade fair in 1988. Kayhan Tehranchi, the young, Iranian-born, British-educated owner of Elika, had ambitious plans for his company. He wanted to become "an American Danese," referring to a famed Italian philanthropist-manufacturer noted for his collaborations with the most respected figures of Italian design.

By a measure of good luck, my first design for Elika became a commercial hit. The stainless steel Laborious Clock was a characteristic late-eighties object: sleek, upscale, and ironic. (More than once, the clock appeared in films where the ambiance of a yuppie loft had to be re-created.) Each number of the clock face was expressed as a different industrial process: the metal sheet was bent, punched, riveted, scratched, and welded. Laborious Clock brought the studio our first I.D. Magazine Design Award. Soon its design was copied, with variations, by several foreign companies.

The success of this first commission gave us a certain freedom to push for more unusual design objects. Mona Lisa Clock originated as a much-publicized exhibition piece. The iconic image appears complete only twice a day: at midday and at midnight. The clock was appreciated as a startling and funny commentary on time and timelessness, a conversation piece with clear references to avant-garde art history. Produced carefully and expensively as a photo transfer on aluminum, this clock was also successful on the market.

"The world does not need any more designer clocks, but I'd be willing to make room for this one."
—Larry Keeley, I.D. Annual Design Review

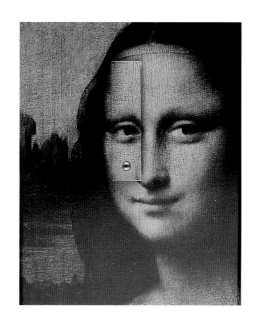

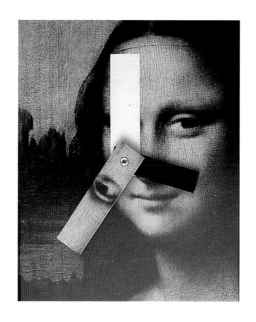

It is hard to understand why a clock was such an important design item around 1990. Yet at the time it seemed the market appetite for design clocks was insatiable. Our experiments with clocks resulted in some highly unusual pieces. Moving Clock, produced by Elika in 1991, was essentially a pendulum. Only the center remained stationary; the rest of the clock face slightly moved in perpetual rocking motion. On the wall, this clock created a funny—and disquieting for some—impression of an animate object.

Salt and pepper shakers—a ubiquitous tabletop couple—were
considered quite literally in this design of Male/Female,
produced in 1992. Special aluminum extrusions were made
in two colors: bronze and silver, the colors of pepper and salt.
My original proposal was to sell them as singles, to allow for
same-sex couples to make their own pairs. This marketing
concept was rejected as too risky.

ELIKA

The recession of the early 1990s hit small design companies hard. Suddenly, expensive stainless steel clocks were no longer selling. A special design brief from Elika requested an item that could retail for under $15. In addition, they had no money to invest in molds, hence no use of plastic was possible.

Staple Clock was made out of cardboard and twelve common staples. We saw staples as beautiful little jewel-like objects that people never had time or habit to notice. By placing them in an unusual context, on a clock face, we were able to attract attention to their decorative quality. Elika produced the clock in 1993 in Los Angeles, where it was stapled by hand with the help of a special template, and offered it on the market for as little as $12.50 retail. Staple Clock was included in an important exhibition, Mutant Materials in Contemporary Design, at MoMA in 1995, where it became a runaway bestseller at the museum shop.

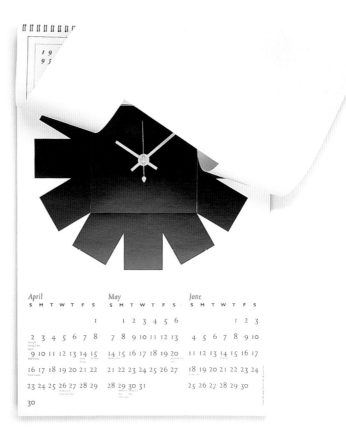

April								May								June						
S	M	T	W	T	F	S		S	M	T	W	T	F	S		S	M	T	W	T	F	S
						1			1	2	3	4	5	6						1	2	3
2	3	4	5	6	7	8		7	8	9	10	11	12	13		4	5	6	7	8	9	10
9	10	11	12	13	14	15		14	15	16	17	18	19	20		11	12	13	14	15	16	17
16	17	18	19	20	21	22		21	22	23	24	25	26	27		18	19	20	21	22	23	24
23	24	25	26	27	28	29		28	29	30	31					25	26	27	28	29	30	
30																						

Another example of "recession design" was Calendar Clock, first produced in 1995. Eminently practical and inexpensive, this combination of a clock and a calendar was originally supposed to have twelve faces, one for each month. (For economic reasons, the number of pages was later reduced to four. Even though design companies have a notoriously difficult time selling calendars, this clock was reissued for three consecutive years.

In spite of its successful line of products, Elika was struggling financially throughout the 1990s. One of their unfortunate cost-cutting measures was an indefinite deferment of designers' royalties. Our relationship soured, and we terminated it in 1997, after almost ten years of collaboration.

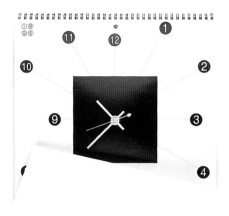

October

S	M	T	W	T	F	S		S	M	T	W	T	F	S		S	M	T	W	T	F	S
1	2	3	4	5	6	7				1	2	3	4							1	2
8	9	10	11	12	13	14		5	6	7	8	9	10	11		3	4	5	6	7	8	9
15	16	17	18	19	20	21		12	13	14	15	16	17	18		10	11	12	13	14	15	16
22	23	24	25	26	27	28		19	20	21	22	23	24	25		17	18	19	20	21	22	23
29	30	31						26	27	28	29	30				24	25	26	27	28	29	30
																31						

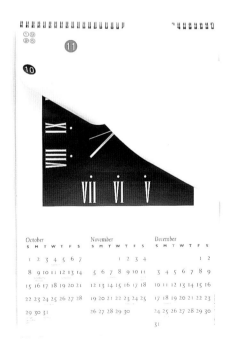

October

S	M	T	W	T	F	S
1	2	3	4	5	6	7
8	9	10	11	12	13	14
15	16	17	18	19	20	21
22	23	24	25	26	27	28
29	30	31				

November

S	M	T	W	T	F	S
			1	2	3	4
5	6	7	8	9	10	11
12	13	14	15	16	17	18
19	20	21	22	23	24	25
26	27	28	29	30		

December

S	M	T	W	T	F	S
					1	2
3	4	5	6	7	8	9
10	11	12	13	14	15	16
17	18	19	20	21	22	23
24	25	26	27	28	29	30
31						

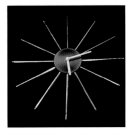

Original prototype of Antenna Clock (folded)

Products for
MORPHOS

In the 1980s, American designers were largely unknown in Europe, and they generated much curiosity. Having settled down in New York, I wrote to a number of Italian manufacturers, many of whom responded enthusiastically. One of them, Lodovico Acerbis, the owner of Morphos and Acerbis International, soon materialized at the door of my studio. He was so taken by the design of Antenna Clock that he took the prototype back to Italy with him, and manufactured it in a record three months' time.

The clock, designed in 1989, continued our exploration of the conventional anonymous object started in the Recycle project. As before, the aim was to redeem the everyday thing (in this case, a standard antenna) from the oblivion and indifference caused by habitual use. Twelve telescopic antennas marked the hours around the clock face. In seconds, the object could grow from eighteen inches to almost six feet in diameter. Depending on the owner's temperament and on available wall space, the clock could be a symmetrical composition or an expressive visual statement. Such inherent object transformation made possible through simple user participation was met with praise by design critics. The clock remained in production for twelve years.

"By shifting objects and fragments from a context in which they are customary to another in which they appear incongruous and unexpected, Boym releases them from their original function, turning conventionality into amused surprise and inviting more careful observation."
—Marta Laudani, Domus

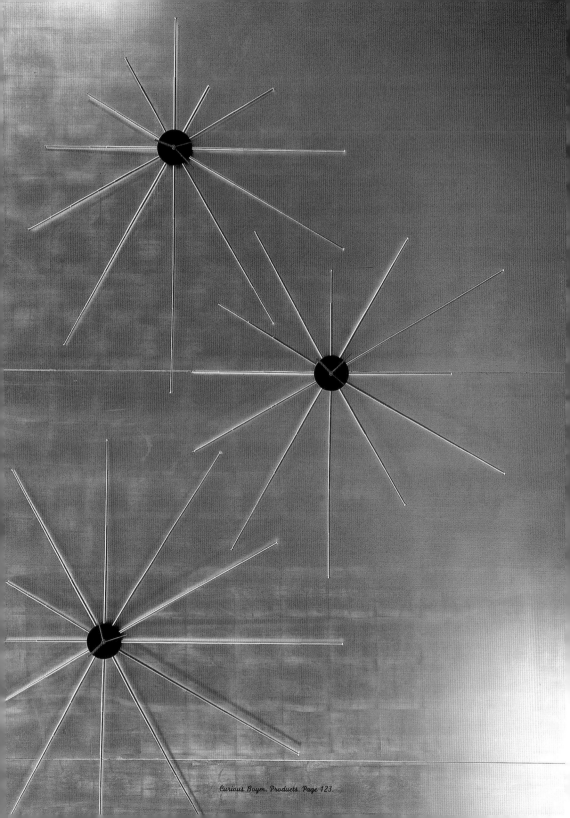

A theme with variations: designs from the Tin Can collection (above and overleaf)

Products for ALESSI

I have always considered a coffee can a beautiful design object. The corrugated body of a standard tin can simultaneously provides structural strength, a decorative pattern, and a tactile gripping surface. A good example of object archetype, today's can has changed very little since the mid-nineteenth century. Having used cans in our Recycle project, we continued variations on the theme until we developed a large set of tabletop objects. Depending on the new objects' function, the cans appeared stretched, flattened, enlarged, or shrunken in size.

In 1990, Alessi was an undisputed leader in producing remarkable stainless steel design objects. In my mind, no other company would have been more perfect to undertake the Tin Can project. The imprimatur and craftsmanship of Alessi seemed essential for turning the humble tin can into a potential design icon. It took three years and several meetings with Alberto Alessi to get him sufficiently excited in the idea. Eventually, only one object from the line, kitchen canisters, was mass-marketed. The final product was edited by the company to appear more sleek and, perhaps, more commercially viable.

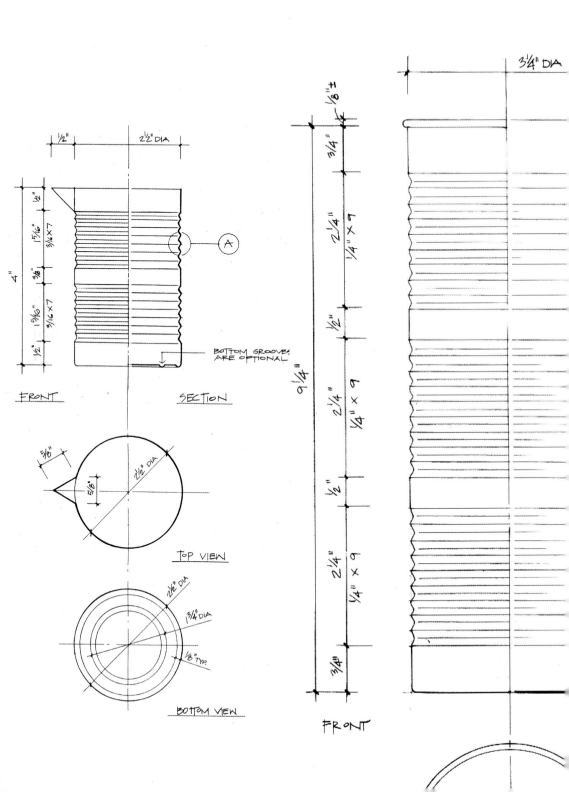

½" 2½" DIA

4" ½" 1⁵⁄₁₆" 3⁄₁₆ × 7 ³⁄₈" 1⁵⁄₁₆" 3⁄₁₆ × 7 ½"

FRONT

A

SECTION

BOTTOM GROOVES
ARE OPTIONAL

⁵⁄₈" 5⁄8" 2½" DIA

TOP VIEW

2½" DIA
3⁄₄" DIA
⅛" TYP.

BOTTOM VIEW

⅛" ± 3⁄₄" 2¼" 1⁄₄" × 9 ½" 2¼" 1⁄₄" × 9 ½" 2¼" 1⁄₄" × 9 3⁄₄"

9¼"

FRONT

3¼" DIA

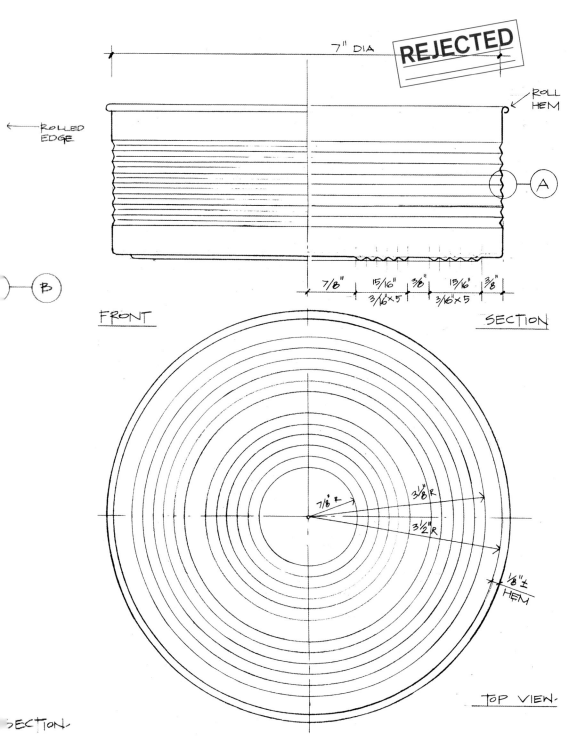

7" DIA

REJECTED

ROLL HEM

← ROLLED EDGE

A

B

7/8" 15/16" 3/8" 15/16" 3/8"
3/16"×5   3/16"×5

FRONT

SECTION

7/8" R   3 1/8" R

3 1/2" R

1/8" ± HEM

TOP VIEW·

SECTION·

The success of the canisters generated a good response at Alessi. In 1993 they asked us to continue the work in the direction of "anonymous" design. "I would like to create some industrial 'types,'" wrote Alberto Alessi. "They are, I know, common objects in the American culture. They could have excellent chances also in Europe." We started the work with great enthusiasm.

The new collection comprised a group of items one would find on the table of any roadside diner. While the objects retained an air of familiarity, there was always a twist to them. In one proposal, we inverted the materials, with bodies drawn of stainless steel and lids molded in clear plastic. In a second, more realistic proposal, the objects were "almost all right," to quote Robert Venturi, but their proportions appeared scaled up and slimmed down.

Alessi responded to our design presentation in Milan with a round of applause, and the company began work on prototypes immediately. After several weeks of almost daily communication we started to sense a turnaround. The project soon stopped, without any explanations given.

REJECTED

Products for
SWATCH

In 1995 I paid a visit to the legendary Milanese designer Alessandro Mendini, my former employer and mentor from my years at Domus Academy. At the time, Mendini was responsible for the art direction of Swatch. Having looked at our clock designs, he suggested we submit a project for the Swatch "artists' edition." "I'll tell them you are an artist," he said with a wink.

The brief for the watch limited our interventions to pictorial images on the dial and on the band. In order to make the design more three-dimensional, we found a new application for a lens normally used to enlarge the date on the dial. We placed six such lenses over numbers, encoded as miniature icons of everyday life, and centered the seventh on the movement itself. "Let's look at the world with fresh eyes, with inquisitiveness and humor," read the note that accompanied our submission. Before the final approval, Swatch Lab in Milan carefully reviewed all our icons. In a strange twist, they deemed the six-pack "too American," and we had to be replace it with a more neutral symbol, six pencils.

The watch, issued in an edition of 50,000 in the summer of 1996, was hugely popular and sold out within weeks of production.

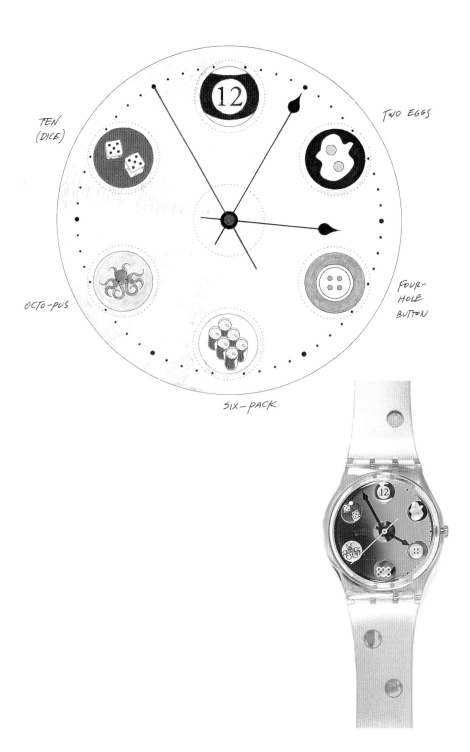

TEN
(DICE)

TWO EGGS

OCTO-PUS

FOUR-
HOLE
BUTTON

SIX – PACK

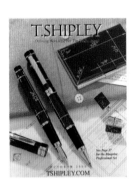

Blueprint for success: by 2000, the Blueprint objects were a hit in mail-order catalogs and in-flight magazines around the country

Products for
ACME

In 1998 we received a letter from Acme Studios in Maui, Hawaii, with an invitation to decorate a pen. Adrian Olabuenaga and Lesley Bailey, Acme's owners, had already collaborated with many great names in architecture and design, realizing their ambitious vision to build up the "Swatch of the pen business."

For our studio, with no proper "signature" style, such decorative projects are never easy. After much deliberation, I proposed a pattern that is not a decoration at all. The design simply repeats the dimensions of the basic template, rendering them in a traditional architect's handwriting. This combination of dead-pan irony and inherent nostalgia of the blueprint found strong resonance with architects and their friends, the main customer group of Acme Studios. The Blueprint pattern became the biggest commercial success in the history of the company. Soon, the pen was followed by a card case, a watch, a set of notebooks, and even cufflinks and a tie.

When the American Institute of Architects placed a huge order for the Blueprint pens for their annual convention, I remembered how in 1981 I was nearly fired from my first architectural job in Boston for not being able to do the proper architect's lettering.

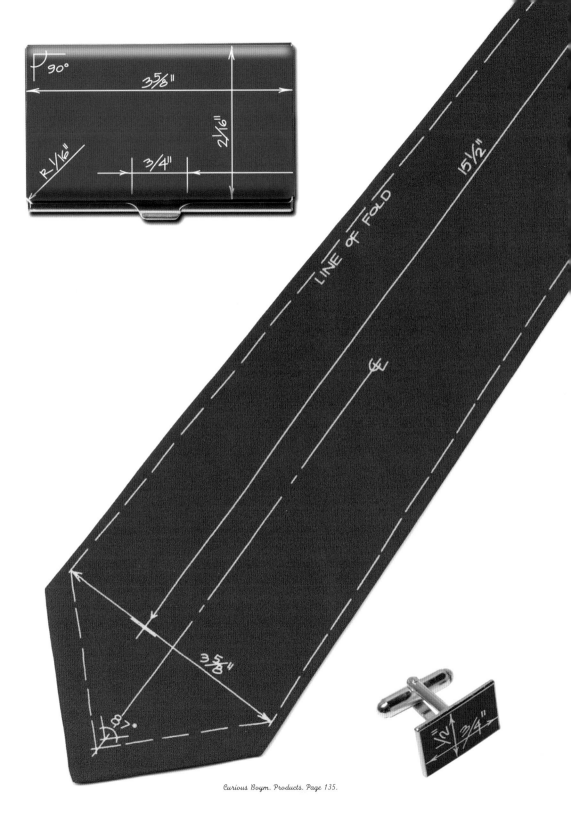

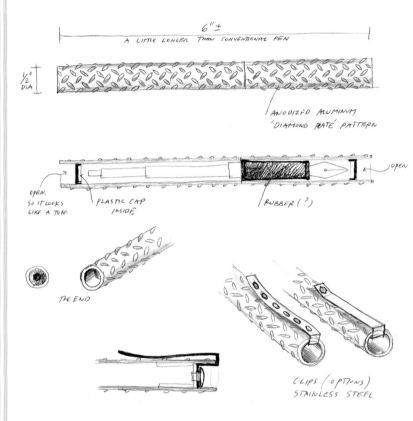

6" ±
A LITTLE LONGER THAN CONVENTIONAL PEN

½" DIA

ANODIZED ALUMINUM 'DIAMOND PLATE' PATTERN

OPEN, SO IT LOOKS LIKE A TUBE

PLASTIC CAP INSIDE

RUBBER (?)

OPEN

THE END

CLIPS (OPTIONS) STAINLESS STEEL

Our next pen for Acme was a more ambitious project. No longer a decoration of a preexisting body, this pen was designed as a simple tube with a texture of diamond-plate steel. By referencing this common industrial pattern we wanted to create a feeling of downtown New York. By happy coincidence, diamond plate turned out to be Adrian Olabuenaga's favorite material; he already used it for Acme's display furniture and signage. "With this pattern, it was a foregone conclusion that we were going to do it, the question was how and when," he wrote. But soon we learned that producing a seamless tube with a diamond-plate surface was virtually impossible. We poured over pen catalogs in search for a solution. Noticing pens with etched caps, we suggested doing the acid etching in reverse, removing the background instead of the pattern itself. This technique proved so innovative that Acme had it patented in China.

In the 1940s, glass refrigeratorware was often included as a gift with the purchase of a new refrigerator. Today, these pieces are highly collectible.

"Of all products the Boyms have done for Authentics, the plastic container set 'Use It' is my favorite product. Nothing about this set is extremely special or new, yet it has the quality of an unmistakable design icon. It shows knowledge of all these container boxes designed in the last 40 years."
—Hans Maier-Aichen

"I had come to believe that it was not the designer's job to invent form, just to apply it in the right places at the right time and for good enough reasons."
—Jasper Morrison, Everything but the Walls

Products for

AUTHENTICS

One of our most important collaborations of the 1990s took place with the German company Authentics. The company's owner, Hans Maier-Aichen, was a successful minimalist sculptor before he applied his training and beliefs in the unlikely field of manufacturing and design. Guided by Zen-like principles like "The more you know, the less you need," Authentics became known for products made of translucent polypropylene, striking in their thinness, fine texture, and luminous color effects.

Our first meeting with Maier-Aichen took place in Frankfurt during the Searstyle exhibition. Impressed with the project, he suggested we try our hand on the subject of Tupperware. His finalized brief called for a universal set of plastic containers. "Make them more than simple," urged Maier-Aichen. The containers had to become dignified enough to escape a cheap connotation of kitchen objects, to find use in the bathroom, bedroom, even office. Our work on the project attempted to simplify and eliminate every unnecessary articulation or detail. In the end, our series of modular toy-like blocks looked almost generic, reminiscent of Wilhelm Wagenfeld's glass cubes or the American refrigeratorware of the 1940s. New was their immaterial lightness and ethereal translucent colors, which the company changed every season.

Issued in 1995, "Use It" containers were a big critical and commercial success, even though they raised a few eyebrows regarding their presumed "absence of design." This question was put to rest three years later when the containers were accepted into the permanent design collection of the Museum of Modern Art in New York.

1940s American utensils with
red handles make up some
prized collections today

Have a Happy Kitchen! Boym
Holiday card, 1996

Authentics' design brief for kitchen utensils began with a
challenge. The products' material, heat-resisting polyamide,
could only be made black, which did not suit the signature
Authentics palette of translucent polypropylene colors. On flea
market trips we had encountered 1940s American steel utensils,
distinguished by their brightly colored wooden handles. These
collectible objects offered us a clue. Instead of wood and steel,
we combined two kinds of plastic, their connection carefully
engineered to appear almost immaterial.

The shapes of the objects were worked out to look reassuringly
familiar. A small and slim handle served as a decorative
signifier, contrary to the tendency of oversized, expressively
ergonomic handles, hardly necessary for the delicate task of
ladling soup. "The bigger the handle, you know, the bigger the
ego," commented Laurene in an interview with the *New York
Times*.

Issued in 1996, the utensils had a successful run at Target.
However, the limitations of Authentics' distribution began to
surface. A small set of three objects had little chance
competing with a full line offered by other companies.

A good thing: wall mirror on a silk ribbon

In 1997 Authentics expanded its product lines into the field of furnishings. We received a very specific brief for a hanging wall mirror: almost everything in it, including its size, circular shape, and price point, was predetermined by marketing considerations. It seemed the only thing left open was a way of attaching it to the wall. As chance would have it, that month's *Martha Stewart Living* magazine ran an article on "classy" ways of hanging a mirror. Inspired by her silk ribbon suggestions, we proposed a wraparound plastic ribbon that would both house the glass and provide a loop for hanging. This design combined a minimally functional solution with the playful irreverence of a cartoon.

While Authentics acknowledged minimalism as the company's artistic credo, Maier-Aichen has always had enough creative freedom to embrace humor, character, and "ugliness," which for him was often an exultant term.

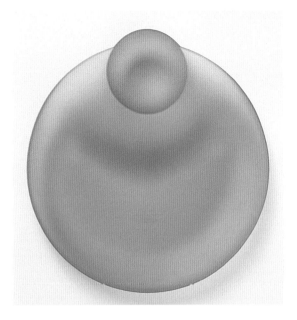

Our designs for Authentics often referred to traditional American product types, such as disposable sectional plates and collectible baskets.

Hans Maier-Aichen has always maintained that America was a country with an honest and unprejudiced mass market ideology. From our first introduction at the Searstyle exhibition, Maier-Aichen valued our "very American way of consuming and at the same time criticizing the consumer lifestyle." Most of our products for Authentics commented on traditional American typologies, such as our Chip-n-Dip plate of 1996, an updated version of sectional plates and TV dinner trays.

We designed Bath Caddy in 1997 as a part of Authentics' move towards more sophisticated plastic products. Attempting to create a nice personal object, we turned to traditional handmade baskets, with their characteristic proportions and woven patterns. We included a flat, removable tray for smaller bath items; it could be used elsewhere in the bathroom.

Introduced on the market in 1998, Bath Caddy illuminated Authentics' dilemma. While their products were more sophisticated and often better designed, they were also more expensive: a condition that most consumers were not willing to accept. The company suffered from indiscriminate knockoffs and competitive products that eventually eroded the market for translucent plastic goods. Their attempts to diversify their production into other materials were not immediately successful. In 2000, Authentics declared bankruptcy. After six years of work and twelve marketed products, we ended up with nothing. But we still have lunch with Hans Maier-Aichen when he is in town.

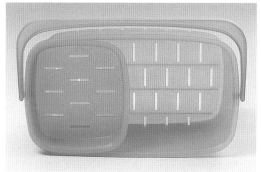

Products for

BENZA

During years of collaboration with Authentics, we accumulated a lot of designs that were put aside to wait for future opportunities. One of these was a trio of bath accessories titled "Cloud Nine." We worked hard to create objects with an "almost non-design" quality: the final product resembled enigmatic parts that could belong to an electrical substation. On closer look, the strange pieces worked surprisingly well as holders for soap and toothbrushes.

In 1998, we developed Cloud Nine for Benza, a small design company founded in New York City by Laurene's classmates from Pratt, Giovanni Pellone and Bridget Means. Production pieces were cast in bonded marble, a combination of epoxy resin and marble dust, commonly associated with souvenir manufacturing. The physical and tactile qualities of this economical material proved to work well in the context of the bathroom.

Cloud Nine, a common term in American popular culture, emerged as a slang idiom sometime during the 1950s. It means completely happy, perfectly satisfied, and slightly out of touch with one's surroundings.

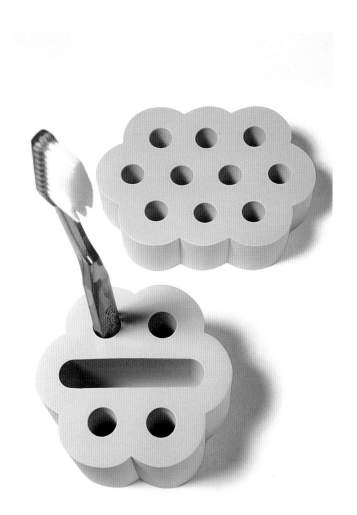

Happy recipients of American Plumbing (Steven and Mara Skov Holt)

Once, while lost in the aisles of a large suburban hardware store, we stumbled upon shelves full of plumbing PVC fittings, strangely beautiful in their white sculptural expression. Marcel Duchamp's oft-quoted statement, "The only works of art America has given are her plumbing and her bridges," suddenly acquired a new meaning. We assembled our first American Plumbing flower vases in a true "readymade" fashion, using proper PVC parts and plumber's adhesive.

In 1999, Jasper Morrison selected the vases for his edition of *International Design Yearbook* and we exhibited them in New York. Soon, Benza made a surprising offer to put the objects in production, in spite of my reservations about their commercial viability. I still find a special pleasure in bringing one of these vases to a friend's or a relative's birthday celebration, and watching their reaction when they open the present.

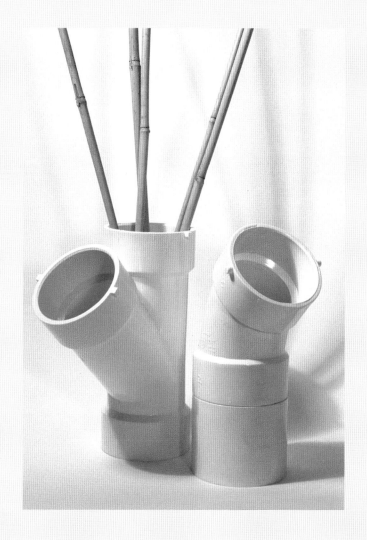

Products for
DMD

The Dutch company DMD (Development Manufacturing Distribution) was founded in 1993 in close relationship with a notorious design collective known as Droog Design. "Act normally, and that's crazy enough," a traditional Dutch saying, has become the operative mode of Droog Design. The group's much-publicized projects ingeniously interpreted conventional objects, unexpectedly subverting their materials and textures. For its part, DMD was concerned with production, trying to bring at least some of Droog's innovative ideas into the marketplace.

Needless to say, the Droog mentality felt very dear to us. A strange sensation of being "separated at birth" was acknowledged when Droog included early Boym projects into the introduction of their first monograph. In retrospect, I was not so surprised when in 1998 we received a fax from Teake Bulstra, the owner of DMD, inviting us to contribute designs to their product line. "Now is the time to extend the collection with a number of products called 'basics,'" wrote Bulstra. "A parallel might be drawn with top fashion collections combining outstanding models with basic garments." Following the guidelines of "translating familiar everyday activities and objects into our modern age," we sent a portfolio of proposals to Amsterdam.

"I like products that are rooted in things that already exist, only realized in another material and another size, and in another context."
—*Ed Annink*

"Why invent a new form when there already is one suitable in every respect?"
—*Renny Ramakers*

GLASS STACK

I AM ALWAYS FASCINATED BY STACKS OF
PLASTIC GLASSES AT A PARTY.

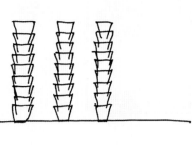

IT IS A BEAUTIFUL AND
ECONOMICAL WAY
TO DISPLAY CONVENTIONAL
OBJECTS.

BUT IT IS BETTER NOT
TO DO IT WITH GOOD GLASS
AT HOME:

THE STACK IS VERY UNSTABLE

I WOULD LIKE TO PROPOSE A SPECIAL SET
OF STACKING GLASSES (FOR WATER, VINE, MILK...)

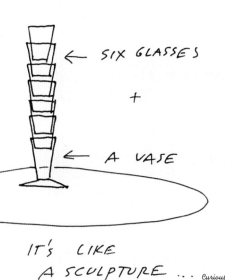

← SIX GLASSES

+

← A VASE

IT'S LIKE
A SCULPTURE ...

WHICH INSTANTLY
TURNS INTO A PARTY!

SUSPENDED JARS

THERE EXISTS A SMART AMERICAN DO-IT-YOURSELF WAY
TO STORE SCREWS, NUTS, BOLTS IN THE WORKSHOP.

PEOPLE TAKE AN EMPTY MAYONNAISE JAR
ATTACH ITS LID UNDER THE SHELF;
THEN THE JAR CAN BE TWISTED
IN AND OUT, AND USED FOR
STORAGE.

IT SAVES SPACE!

WE SUGGEST TO MAKE A SPICE RACK
BASED ON THE SAME PRINCIPLE:

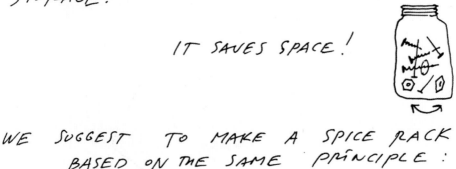

CABINETS

THEY APPEAR
SUSPENDED IN
THE AIR!

RIVET (?)

METAL STRIP
INTEGRATED
WITH METAL
TWIST-ON LID

PLASTIC SIFTER

CLEAR GLASS
SPICE JARS
[EXISTING
READY-MADE
CONTAINERS
COULD BE USED]

COUNTER

DMD was intrigued by this idea, and the spice rack was produced the following year. This remarkably practical product never fails to surprise visitors to our kitchen.

PAPER TABLES

WE ALL KNOW BLOCKS OF PAPER, USED FOR
WRITING NOTES:

COAT
OF GLUE

NIKE

THERE IS
OFTEN A LO
IMPRINTED
ON THE SIDE

THESE ARE NICE, USEFUL OBJECTS.

WHAT IF THE PAPER BLOCK IS THE SIZE
OF A TABLE?

ONE CAN WRITE, DRAW, DOODLE ON IT; THEN RENE
THE SURFACE BY TEARING OFF THE TOP SHEET.
THE SHEETS COULD BE PRESERVED. THIS IDEA ALSO
REFERS TO PAPER TABLECLOTH, USED IN SOME
POPULAR CAFÉS.

PAPER SIZE A2
MAKES A GOOD
COFFEE TABLE →

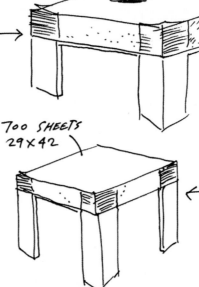

1000 SHEE
60×42

COAT
OF GLUE
ALL 4
SIDES,
EXCEPT
IN CORNERS

1/2"
MD.

700 SHEETS
29×42

500 SHEETS
21×29

← A3
IS A SMALLE
SIDE TABLE

← A4 IS A TABLETOP OBJECT:
A WRITING TABLET FOR DESKTOP

DMD called this proposal "just an idea," and requested we give it a certain clearly defined function and parameters. Eventually, we redesigned the piece in galvanized steel sheet for use as a telephone table. A specially produced block of paper and pencils were included with each product. Once the paper is finished, it is up to the owner to renew the block or to find for the table a new use as occasional or bedside furniture.

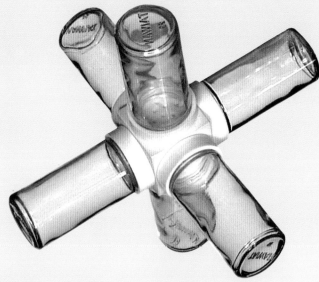

Products for

READYMADE

We designed Spice Station in 1998, in the midst of our work on the DMD product proposals. We turned an anonymous do-it-yourself storage concept, commonly found in an American garage, into a three-dimensional tabletop object. Almost incidentally, the finished set ended up looking like a space station. The working prototype generated interest from one manufacturer, then another, but no commitment followed.

In 2001 we got a call from *ReadyMade*, an emerging magazine from Berkeley, with an unusual request. This new publication, a witty and energetic proponent of do-it-yourself culture, was to provide on its pages actual instructions for making objects of everyday life. They asked if we could contribute an interesting design recipe for their first issue. We were happy to volunteer the instructions for making the Spice Station. A design that originated as people's know-how has now returned back to the public domain. Please make one at home.

×6

2. 2"x2"x2"
WOOD CUBE

1. STANDARD
SPICE
CONTAINER

1. For the project you will need six identical generic glass spice containers with flat plastic or metal lids. A plastic sifter is usually provided as a part of such containers. These objects can be found in discount housewares stores for about $1 apiece.

2. Make or find a solid wood cube approximately two inches square. Your little brother's or sister's wood block can be reused for this purpose. Tell them to share.

3. Attach a lid from the container to one side of the cube with at least two small screws. If the block is hardwood, predrilling holes is advisable.

4. Repeat the operation five times so that each side of the block has a lid attached. Your connector is now finished.

5. Fill containers with salt, pepper, and your other favorite spices. Simply twist containers into their lids. The Spice Station is ready for launch.

×6

3. ASSEMBLY

4. FINISHED CONNECTOR

SALT

PEPPER

PAPRIKA

ETC

5. SPICE STATION

Products for
HANDY

"The glowing icons mimic the way these products are seen on neon signs, and they have been woven in phosphorescent yarn to replicate the brilliance of neon at night."
—George H. Marcus, What Is Design Today?

Glowing rolls of phosphorescent yarn looked like props from the Superman movie.

The origins of Handy, our own new company and brand, were predictably serendipitous. It all started with one unusual object, Glow Rug, created for an exhibition on decoration in early 2001. Most likely, this was the first rug made with phosphorescent yarn, originally formulated for emergency exit signage. Exposure to daylight or electric light enabled the outlines of the pattern to glow gently at night. Our application of this new technology to a decorative rug allowed for a new relationship with a familiar domestic object. With a bit of irony, the decor itself—a pattern of old-fashioned, generic, nondescript appliances—also invoked technology.

The rug generated much interest, publicity, and requests for more exhibitions. Murray Moss, the owner of a famed design shop in SoHo, expressed interest in carrying it in his store. Production of the rugs was straightforward: the pieces were made in New Jersey in a friendly shop that agreed to produce them on demand. Suddenly, we felt a new opportunity, a chance to take matters into our own hands. The experiences of young European designers such as Hella Jongerius and our friend Marcel Wanders, who in recent years had taken over the production of their designs, was an important inspiration for our company.

We called the new company "Handy" to emphasize its inherent connection with handicrafts. From the outset we decided to concentrate on experimental products, on objects with sophisticated cultural content, superior quality, and high prices (the only possibility for a small enterprise). We were not concerned with straightforward functionalism, but wanted to offer objects for emotional fulfillment, items for collectors and connoisseurs (we had had a good experience with this while working on the souvenir catalog). One more rule applied, unofficially: the designs had to be unusual enough that bringing them to any other manufacturer would be simply futile.

From Egyptian temples to roadside stands, animals remain the world's oldest and most popular decoration

Surprisingly, many buyers were less interested in the glow-in-the-dark aspect of the rugs than in their overall decorative impact. For the first Handy collection of 2001 we decided to forego the phosphorescent yarn in favor of more conventional fluorescent colors. The collection consisted of several small throw rugs with animal figures, the most ancient decoration known to humankind. These animals were interpreted in Laurene's peculiar graphic style, which combines the precision of pictograms with the deliberate naivete of a child's drawing. The rug's texture had a three-dimensional quality, as some surfaces were sheared, some looped, and some left as a shag. Making the rugs combined computer technology (the drawings were computer generated and transferred onto looms) with hand tufting and shearing. Such technology-based, manually executed objects delineate the future direction of Handy.

Handy's animal rugs were praised as a fresh look at nursery products, an area where few contemporary designers have ventured. Unfortunately, high manufacturing costs pushed the rugs beyond the price range of most households. More than once, they were called "art for the floor." Transferring production to India, we are trying to turn these high-end decorative objects into products for daily family use.

VITRA SHOWROOM

Chicago, Merchandise Mart

Every year in June, Neocon, the largest American trade fair of contract furniture, takes place at Merchandise Mart in Chicago, where hundreds of showrooms compete for the attention of many thousands of visitors. For the event, all showrooms get a facelift, and many undertake a complete redesign. In the spring of 1999, Vitra USA, prompted by the request of their Swiss owner Rolf Fehlbaum, asked us to provide a new design for their two small spaces. The client characterized their current nondescript white spaces as "too cold," and we were requested to "warm it up" with a fast and low-budget intervention.

The next night, at our son's bedtime, we followed the adventures of Harold, a persistent little character who created all his environments by sketching them in the air with his purple crayon. This classic children's story suggested an idea of simply drawing the new showroom on the walls, windows, and floors of the old one. Eventually, the drawings were done on the Mac, produced as computer output on black adhesive vinyl, and applied directly to the showroom's surfaces. A collection of colorful plastic chairs on display appeared as if inside of a three-dimensional black-and-white drawing.

Drawing of a room by Bobby Boym, age 5

The drawings celebrated the conventional components of architectural interiors: windows, doorways, flower pots, fire sprinklers. Our message was that even sophisticated Vitra furniture lives in a "real" world. By adding outlines of a fireplace, a heating radiator, and a puppy, we followed Vitra's request to warm up the space, almost literally.

During the installation we learned about the requirement of showroom styling. Typically this involves a thoughtful placement of pretty vases, pencil holders, candy dishes, and such, which are supposed to make the showroom look inhabited. Instead, we opted for a bolder option. Together with Andrew Goetz, a manager of the project, we made a trip to a local supermarket, where we got a large selection of cleaning supplies. We placed color-coordinated compositions of detergents, paper towels, brushes, and brooms among the furniture, as if they had been forgotten there by a cleaning crew.

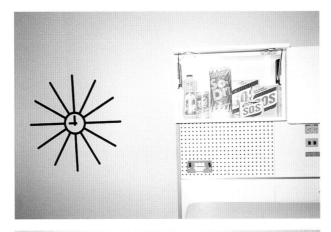

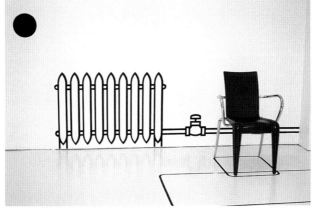

The full effect of the Vitra showroom design could only be appreciated in the context of other Neocon presentations. In the middle of serious, self-gratifying, and expensive interiors, our environment stood out in every possible respect. I watched people hurry along the building's endless corridors, glance at the Vitra display, and stop with a smile. Then they would slowly make their way in as if lured by the Pied Piper.

Design critics praised the showroom design as an example of an economical solution, "a challenge to the $12 billion-per-square-foot mentality." In 2000, the Vitra showroom was voted Best of Category at the I.D. Annual Design Review. "This project shows that you can make something where there is an idea and a little simplicity," wrote Walter Chatham in *I.D. Magazine*. The installation was selected for several international yearbooks of best showroom design. So far, the client has not hired us again.

Three components of the urban
playground: pavement, chainlink,
picnic table

CAMPER

Proposal for Camper Store, New York

In the summer of 1999 we received a surprising telephone call
from the hip Spanish shoe company Camper. Its owner, Lorenzo
Fluxa, wanted to talk with us about working on the company's
pilot store in New York City. It became clear during our first
meeting that Camper's understated design sensibility and
offbeat sense of humor were indeed a good match to our
interests and abilities. Fluxa wanted an innovative concept,
a new way of retailing rather than a new look; he envisioned
the store as a magnet for tourists and a feature in lifestyle
magazines. Despite its carefully chosen location on an
exclusive SoHo corner, the store had a budget in line with
Camper's philosophy of economy and casualness.

We attempted to translate the major theme of Camper footwear,
the outdoors, into the urban conditions of New York City. Street
pavement extended directly into the store to give people
a chance to try shoes in almost real conditions. Galvanized
chain-link fences divided the space into functional areas
and provided flexible displays for shoes and accessories.
We completed the urban playground with long picnic tables,
adopted here as store furniture. A standard feature in city
parks, the picnic table appeared well suited for a retail
environment. Its tabletop allowed for varied footwear displays,
while its integrated double bench served for trying on shoes
and socializing.

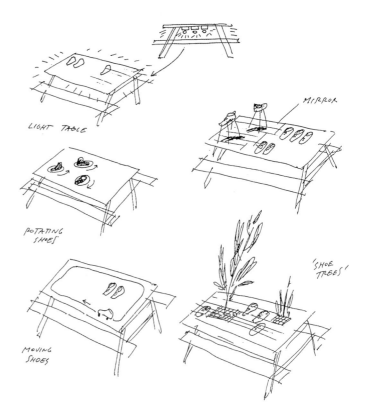

LIGHT TABLE

MIRROR

ROTATING SHOES

'SHOE TREES'

MOVING SHOES

We saw the tabletops as miniature theater stages for ever-changing creative installations, and proposed lights, movement, sculpture, live plants, and stuffed animals for a first group of displays. Shoppers would be drawn into the store, from table to table, as if visiting a museum or an amusement park. In a more radical installation, we floated clouds of shoes suspended on shoe trees in one area of the store.

We envisioned this creative combination of commerce, entertainment, and performance art as a new comprehensive concept for a shopping environment. We felt this approach was appropriate for a store in SoHo, where art galleries have almost completed their exodus. Rem Koolhaas's studies on the convergence of shopping and culture, published two years later, confirmed the validity of our early intent.

Our design presentation in Barcelona generated a long and animated discussion among the company's top players. Since most of the argument was in Catalan, we could only guess at the outcome, but something did not feel right. A week later we received a letter from Lorenzo Fluxa, who canceled the project with great apologies, vaguely hinting at insurmountable politics. Eventually, a much more conventional store opened at the site.

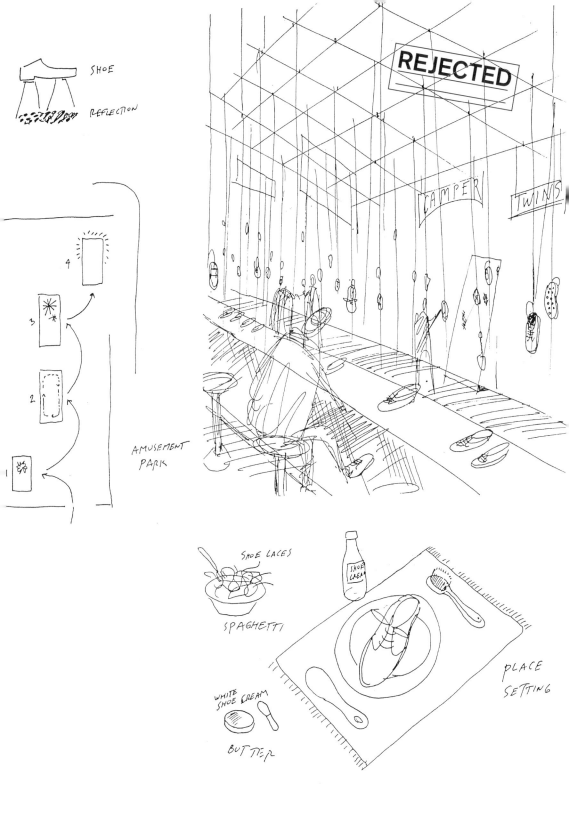

SHOE

REFLECTION

REJECTED

CAMPER

TWINS

AMUSEMENT PARK

4

3

2

1

SHOE LACES

SHOE CREAM

SPAGHETTI

WHITE SHOE CREAM

BUTTER

PLACE SETTING

BED-ROOM

Project for Interiors magazine

At the beginning of 2001 we were asked by the editors of
Interiors magazine to propose a conceptual design for a very
small room in an urban hotel. "Chic hotels are popping up with
guest rooms of ever-shrinking dimensions," wrote the editors.
"Intrigued by the design challenges of a microscopic guest
room, the magazine asked five firms known for exceptional
creativity (though not necessarily for hotel work) to introduce
comfort, luxury, and high-tech amenities in 140 square feet,
including bath."

Through our own extensive traveling we gained enough
experience to tackle this project. The essence of the hotel
room, we realized, was a bed. As a rule, a hotel room is wanted
only when one needs a bed. It is not by chance that the bed is
often the heart of the room, the focal point of the space and its
main interior feature.

In a tiny room the bed could not be compromised. Instead, we
proposed to turn the entire room into a very big canopy bed,
which is traditionally evocative of comfort, luxury, and ease.
Our bed was to be nine by ten feet. On entering, guests would
take off their shoes (a good idea, anyway) and climb on.

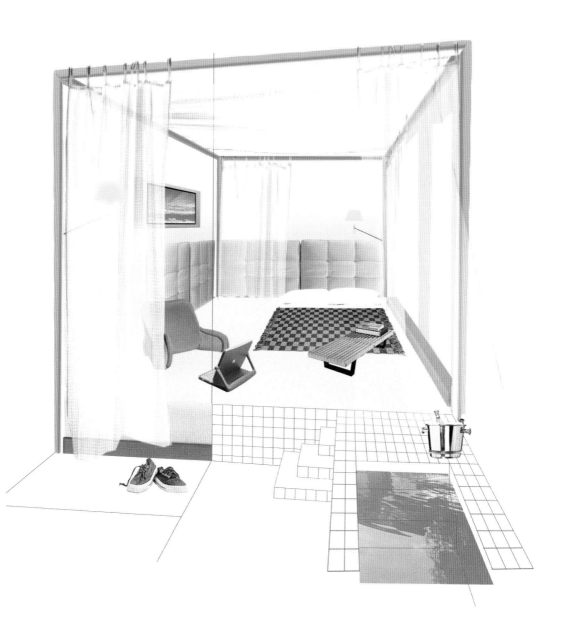

Even though canopy beds are now available through mail-order catalogs, they still signify luxury and comfort

In American households beds are flexible environments, used for a great many activities

Obviously, our Bed-Room would be used for more than sleeping. Americans do a great deal of things in their beds, anyway. In additional to obvious activities, they use it for eating, reading, playing games, watching TV, talking on the phone, and having impromptu family gatherings. In our bed, they could also work, having plugged in their laptops and Palm Pilots.

The bed was directly connected to a bathtub, raised to the same level. Due to limitations of space, we used a Japanese-style sitting tub, another example of compact luxury. Throughout the room, a juxtaposition of traditional and high-tech elements created a contemporary, slightly eclectic, and relaxed feeling.

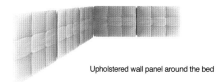

Upholstered wall panel around the bed

Wool comforter and pillows

Translucent curtains

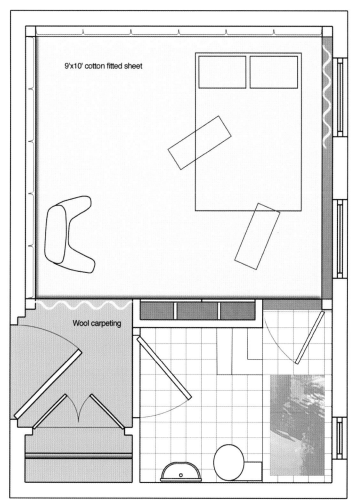

9'x10' cotton fitted sheet

Wool carpeting

Phillips flat screen TV

Sears bedrest

Miniature George Nelson bench as tray table

Japanese style sitting bath

DMD soft polyurethane sink

Ecological toilet (prototype)

BETWEEN FENCES

Exhibition at National Building Museum, Washington D.C.

"We live between fences," wrote curator Greg Dreicer at the beginning of his exhibition. "We may hardly notice them, but they are dominant figures in our lives." The show, opened in 1996, addressed "questions rarely asked—who invented different fence types, how they were built, why they are the way they are, and what meaning they have." For our studio, with our long-time interest in and attention to such overlooked aspects of the American landscape, this subject was an ideal match.

To emphasize the main premise of the exhibition, we proposed to install the show entirely on fences. We believed that in the context of museum galleries, conventional fencing would look strange enough to reawaken visitors' perception and aesthetic appreciation. Traveling from New York to Washington by train, we took notice of endless expanses of chainlink fence stretching along the tracks. Even though chainlink technology originated in Germany, the product was widely used in America since the beginning of the twentieth century, and it truly could be counted among great American icons. For the exhibition, we envisioned transparent layers of chainlink walls for display, circulation, and enclosure. Historical fences and artifacts mounted on a background of chainlink would offer visual collages along with interesting curatorial comparisons.

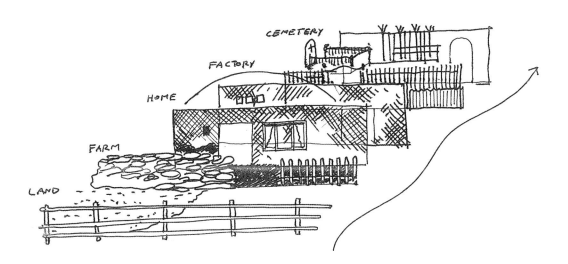

Authentic chainlink fences were installed in the museum
galleries by an enterprising contractor, in a manner similar
to fencing a parking lot. In the show we used chainlink in six
different colors, including rarely seen white and red. The system
proved surprisingly flexible and effective for the exhibition's
purposes. In one gallery, green chainlink served as a protective
screen, preventing the visitors from touching a historical
eighteenth-century "worm" wood fence. In other instances,
it provided surfaces for mounting photographs, texts, and
diagrams. In the main gallery, a huge functional machine for
making chainlink was itself on exhibit, accompanied with patent
drawings. It was calculated that such a machine working for the
duration of the show would produce enough fence to encircle
the entire Washington, D.C. area. The machine on display was
rigged to produce industrial noise and movement rather than
actual product.

The exhibition started with a white picket fence, a traditional symbol of American home and neighborhood. In the final section, the visitors encountered a giant fourteen-foot-high picket fence; they were invited to enter through the pickets. This humorous yet slightly ominous interpretation of the United States boundaries contained displays and information on borders with our two neighbors, Mexico and Canada. To the south there was a fragment of a high wall of interlocking rusted steel sheets; to the north an elegant stainless steel obelisk. "This exhibition is both amusing and bemusing; visitors are unlikely ever to look at fences the same way again," commented the *Washington Post*.

TOLEDO DESIGNS

Alliance of Art and Industry:
Toledo Designs for a Modern America
Exhibition at Toledo Art Museum, Toledo, Ohio

Toledo, Ohio, an All-America City

1940 air compressor made by
the DeVilbiss Company: the
godfather of the Toledo Designs
exhibition

A "Big T" crane, photographed
on a construction site

The city of Toledo, Ohio, is blessed with an exceptionally fine and large art museum. To celebrate its centennial, the museum decided to mount an ambitious exhibition to showcase the city's industrial contribution to American design. First, curator Davira Taragin wanted to test the viability of this idea. In 1997 she assembled a group of design scholars and showed them a selection of photos of potential design artifacts. The group seemed skeptical, until professor John Heskett, looking at an image of a particularly streamlined air compressor, pronounced his verdict: "If a city could produce an appliance like this, it certainly deserves a show."

To obtain artifacts, Taragin tirelessly advertised in the city newspapers, contacted local industries, visited flea markets, and shopped on eBay. Two years later, when our studio joined the team as exhibition designers, the museum had assembled almost 250 objects. Most of these, however, looked like unprepossessing utilitarian things, familiar to people's daily lives. The museum needed a fresh exhibition design approach that could reawaken people's perceptions and turn a journey through Toledo's industrial history into an uplifting experience.

We thought a construction site would be a fitting metaphor for this exhibition. A large construction site is exciting to behold, a busy spectacle of human ingenuity, creativity, and will. The theme and language of construction were explored in many architectural movements throughout the last century, and they were often used in exhibitions and fairs for their symbolism and expressive power. In our exhibition, we interpreted construction in its broadest sense, including the production of ideas, inventions, and designs, as well as the making of buildings and objects. A large T-shaped building crane in the main hall alluded also to the T-square, a once-ubiquitous drafting tool of architects and engineers.

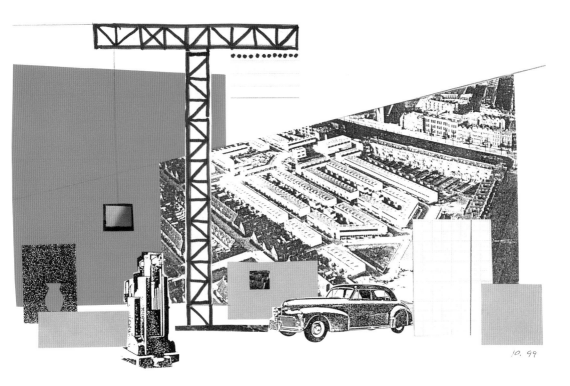

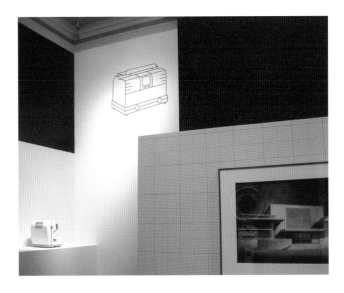

10. 99

The main hall of the Toledo
Designs exhibition

If these are stage sets, they're
of the minimal theater of the
absurd kind: objects positioned
in asymmetrical combinations
like ready-mades in a Dada play.
—Peter Hall, Metropolis

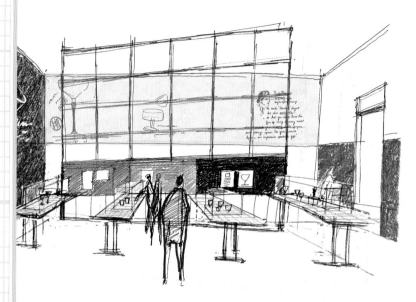

The exhibition combined conventional building materials—steel, plywood, paint, and protective vinyl mesh—with simulated materials evocative of architectural and design studios, like blueprint and graph paper. The latter took on an important presence in the exhibition. We developed and produced a custom plastic laminate with an enlarged graph paper pattern and used it throughout the show.

A design office, often found at large construction sites, was evoked in a display devoted to the emergence of the industrial design profession. Oversized sketches—manifestations of design ideas—appeared on the background of blueprint, yellow tracing paper, and blackboard. We lined presentation tables with graph paper laminate, as if to emphasize the imminent emergence of objects and glassware from designers' drafting boards. Imposing portraits of male industrial design pioneers presided over the room's displays.

We faced an unusual design challenge in presenting one project, Creston Doner's visionary "Kitchen of Tomorrow." This 1942 work heralded new uses for glass and innovative appliances for a servantless family. Only three prototypes of the kitchen were ever made; none of them survived. What remained was a set of optimistic promotional photographs showing a functioning kitchen in minute detail. The museum first suggested that we create a replica, an option we decided not to take due to prohibitive costs and insufficient technical documentation. Instead, we recreated the kitchen as a memory, a blackline drawing on walls and glass partitions. We complemented the drawing with old photos of Doner's kitchen in use, placed directly on top of the wall image, appealing to people's fantasy, imagination, and sense of humor.

Our application of environmental graphics, first used in the design for the Vitra showroom in 1999, here aimed at a new level of sophistication. Instead of providing a complete display, we offer a framework of signifiers and allow people's imaginations to do the rest. A consistent application of this approach should result in installations that respect and encourage the creative abilities of the museum public.

The exhibition's opening in March 2002 was an important cultural and civic affair in the city of Toledo, with the mayor, city councilmen, and other public officials in attendance. The museum's director, Roger Berkowitz, was only half-joking when he said that every Toledo citizen must visit the show. Praising the importance of the museum's undertaking, the *Toledo Blade* added: "But the show is equally impressive—and even more surprising—as an aesthetic experience, daring to showcase mass-produced products as objects of visual beauty, dignity, and gravity." An extraordinary three-year-long creative dialog with curator Davira Taragin resulted in "a successful alliance of scholarship and aesthetics," and in a personal friendship.

Franklin Court in Philadelphia (by Venturi, Rauch and Scott Brown, 1976), where Benjamin Franklin's house was recreated on its former site as a ghosted memory, is one of my favorite buildings and a continuing source of inspiration.

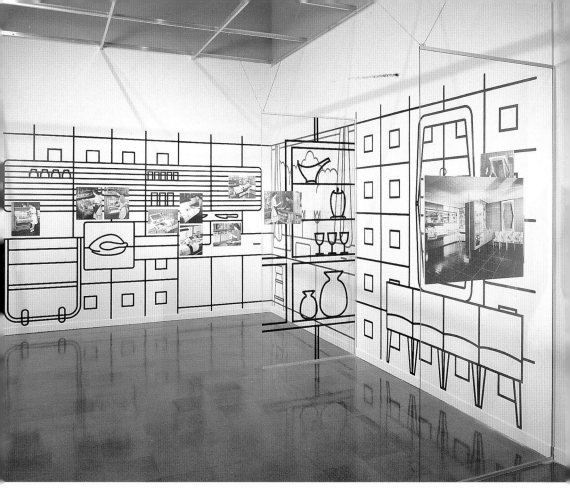

A PERSONAL GATHERING

*Painting and Sculpture from the Collection of
William I. Koch
Exhibition at Wichita Art Museum, Wichita, Kansas*

This large exhibition, designed in 1995–96, began with a formidable set of challenges. William I. Koch, a wealthy and eccentric art collector, asked for an unconventional show. A populist at heart, he wanted to attract the blue-collar families of his hometown Wichita to the art museum, perhaps for the first time, and to offer them an emotional experience they would remember. The show was to express the client's personality and feelings without resorting to the obviousness of photos or video. Above all, he hoped that his very eclectic collection would form a coherent and substantial exhibit.

Curators suggested dividing the artworks into several thematic categories, and we decided to create a different environment for each theme. A walk through the show would thus offer a dramatic, ever-changing experience. The spaces varied in their architectural configurations, in their lighting conditions, and, above all, in their color schemes. It seemed logical to experiment with color in an exhibition of paintings, and so we used some twenty-six different wall colors throughout the galleries. Often, we complemented the artworks with various curious objects from Koch's domestic interior, which I selected from his sprawling home on Cape Cod.

The first large space accommodated Koch's two favorite themes: women and warfare. From a certain angle, one could see miniature cannons aimed at variously rendered women's bodies. This humorous sexual tension was subtle enough to pass unnoticed by most visitors (including the client himself, we hoped).

"I had three exhibitions done for the art critics and for viewers who are accustomed to see art; I have done that. I want to make this exhibition attractive for the people who don't normally see art, for the working class guy rather than the intelligentsia....

"You can take a 1929 boat and put it right next to a 1995 boat and have them both look beautiful and consistent. If it's good art, you can display it in any way, and it still stands out. It's fun to combine things and make an interesting experience out of it....

"I'd like to see this collection jazzed up a bit."

—Bill Koch

A mysterious light-filled opening invited visitors into the next exhibition space. A collection of maritime paintings was exhibited under a brightly lit skylight, which we had uncovered specially for the show after seventeen years of disuse. Sparkling light and various shades of blue gave an impression of being on a ship deck. To add to the effect, we placed several tall ship models and an ancient figurehead sculpture at the end wall.

The passage to the next section of the exhibition, the frontier, was striking. Black and dark green walls surrounded an almost completely dark space. Bronze sculptures by Frederic Remington were installed under spotlights, accompanied by dramatic shadows. Powerful Remington paintings, illuminated with special projection lights, appeared to hover in the darkness.

Exiting from the dark environment of the frontier, visitors found themselves in the middle of a lively display of outdoor sculpture. Natural light, informal picturesque groupings, and a bright green color gave an impression of being in a sun-filled garden. The final section of the exhibition showcased a collection of landscape paintings. This open, expansive area with generously spaced artworks was painted in earthy ocher tones to evoke the spirit of the Kansas plains.

Our design for A Personal Gathering, cautiously accepted by the museum, proved to be an astounding success. In a matter of a few years, our daring and controversial attempt to exhibit art masterpieces on a brightly colored background has become a norm in museums around the country. Many more curators have since sought us out because they wanted "some color" in their exhibitions.

SCREAM THE TRUTH AT THE WORLD

Exhibition at the Museum of Jewish Heritage, New York

Metal box that contained the Ringelblum archive

In the fall of 2001, a collaborative effort between the Jewish Historical Institute in Warsaw, Poland, and the Museum of Jewish Heritage in New York brought a remarkable exhibition to New York City. The exhibition consisted of documents collected by the historian Emmanuel Ringelblum and his colleagues, who were confined in the Warsaw Ghetto from 1940 until its destruction in 1943. On the eve of the Ghetto Uprising, the documents were buried in metal boxes, to be recovered after the war thanks to a handful of survivors. Ringelblum was not among them. A study of his hidden archive proved a truly heart-wrenching experience. Bonnie Gurewitsch, the curator of the exhibition who spent most of her life working with Holocaust materials, confided to me that never before had she seen documents of such emotional impact.

And yet, from a visual point of view, most of the artifacts were small and unprepossessing paper documents, often torn and faded. The challenge of the exhibition design was to command the attention of the visitors, who would arrive at the show at the end of their museum tour, and to make them pause, think, and reflect. Trying to come up with a proper setting, we explored the metaphor of the wall, a sinister and confining barrier that was the most visible manifestation of the Warsaw Ghetto. An eight-foot-high wall was built around the perimeter of an existing gallery space. We presented the artifacts on this wall with an uncommon density, in a seemingly random pattern. The wall had only one interruption, where we displayed the metal box that contained the archive—the single object that escaped the Ghetto's tragic fate.

*Walls of the Warsaw Ghetto in
1940–43*

The exhibition left a particularly strong impression on opening night, when the space was crowded with guests. The dramatic sense of confinement seemed to heighten people's perceptions and emotional tension. Lou Levine, the museum's director of collections and exhibitions, commented on the effect, "The materials, in their white mats, added the only hope and life in the setting, mirroring the hope and life the Jews tried to create in an unfathomable present. The visitor left the exhibit focused on the message of creative possibility even in the presence of unalloyed evil."

Fragments of the JDC archive in the 1960s

TO THE RESCUE

Eight Artists in an Archive
Exhibition at International Center of Photography,
New York

This traveling exhibition was based on the 50,000 photographs preserved in the archive of the American Jewish Joint Distribution Committee (JDC), a humanitarian organization founded in 1914 and still active in bringing relief, rescue, and rehabilitation to millions of people around the globe. The aim of the exhibition project was to reawaken people's memory and sense of history as a way of confirming the organization's never-ending mission of assistance.

Most images in the archive were straightforward documentations of places, people, and events—a far cry from fine art photography. To make these images speak loud and clear, the show's curators, Carole Kismaric and Marvin Heiferman, chose a daring concept. They invited eight different artists—painters, photographers, sculptors, and filmmakers—to spend time in the archive and to turn their impressions into specially created works of art. Our studio, invited as the project's exhibition designer, was given the crucial task of weaving messages of artistic imagination together with images of history into one seamless museum experience.

Familiarizing myself with the JDC archive, I found mysterious photos of anonymous and forbidding rows of file cabinets, as if someone were trying to capture the collection's archetypal essence. We reproduced these photos as giant translucent screens at the entrance to the exhibition. The grim archive suddenly was transparent, open for entry and public scrutiny. Indeed, visitors were invited to go behind the screens to view selections of archival images on several video monitors.

Going through folders of the archive's photographs,
I encountered a great many people's faces—smiling, crying,
frightened, or indifferent; faces of men, women, and children
of all ages and colors. The mission of the JDC was to help
people, and it was clear that people had to become a part of
the exhibition as well. We selected 150 images of individuals
who had been variously affected by the JDC's help, to be
installed as "witnesses" in the gallery space. Many of them
remained unknown, thus the only information printed by each
portrait was the year and the place where the photo was taken.

The witnesses were supposed to populate the exhibition at
all times. During museum hours they would mix with visitors,
and at night they would keep things up, at least symbolically.
A crowd of full-scale figures was first encountered at
the entrance. They continued intermittently throughout
the exhibition space, serving as connecting tissue between
the eight art installations. Each figure was freestanding, which
allowed for a considerable degree of flexibility for traveling
the show to other museum venues.

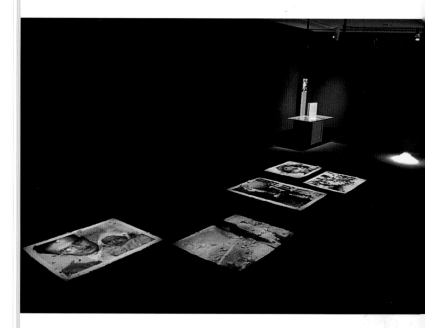

We treated each of the eight artists' photos as "witness" images—after all, they all now became a part of JDC's mission. Each artist was provided a specially designed display table with a glass cover. Here they could exhibit any materials related to their thought and creative process: archival photos, newspaper clippings, sketches, and notes. We decided not to edit these displays from a design point of view; the emphasis was on maximizing their personal expression. We placed each table in a prominent location slightly aside from the artwork, as if the artist was always there on hand, waiting to offer his or her personal commentary.

Installations by Alan Berliner (above) and Magdalena Abakanowicz (right)

At the end of the exhibition, the curators asked for a space devoted to rest and reflection. We proposed a room with sky blue walls, entirely filled with witnesses, to bring the show's theme to its logical conclusion. Here video monitors projected lines of poetry and literary quotations. In this space, exhibition design moved beyond its traditionally assigned limits into the foreground of the visitor's experience. With a bit of irony, Boym was referred to as "the ninth artist" among the curatorial team.

When the exhibition opened in February 1999, it received mixed
reviews. Michael Kimmelman of the *New York Times* called
the show "an interesting failure." For him, the people's images
"did not make a distinct impression....How would it feel
if it were one's own father or daughter or grandmother whose
picture was a decorative effect for people passing through the
installation?" In fact, this was exactly what we were hoping for.
If someone discovered themselves or their loved ones, years later,
commemorated as permanent witnesses to history and art, their
reaction, we were quite sure, would be ecstatic.

MY
McDONALD'S

My first encounter with McDonald's was like a sitcom episode. In 1981, a young and energetic émigré from Moscow, I arrived in Boston. By a stroke of good luck, I quickly managed to get a job at an architectural firm. My biggest desire at the time was to blend in with my new colleagues, to be as normal and socially acceptable as possible for someone who could barely speak—let alone understand—basic English. I noticed that architects would sometimes come back from lunch and tell everyone about a new place to have a good sandwich. This information would usually generate a nice lively conversation. One day at lunchtime, I wandered a little farther from my office than usual. Suddenly I came upon a new, strange restaurant. It was all red and yellow, and very brightly lit. The prices were just right for my wallet. I ordered at random and tasted something I had never tried before: a hamburger, french fries, ketchup.... Back in the office, I made an announcement: "Well, today I found a really great place to have lunch. You guys should all try it, too." "Really? What is it?" several voices asked. "It's called McDonald's," I said proudly. Nobody laughed or said anything funny, but I could see the look on their faces. Something was wrong...

I remembered this story many years later, when the Iron Curtain suddenly started to give in and the first incredulous visitors from the Soviet Union trickled into the West. I was taking one of these overwhelmed guests, my old school friend, on a long walk through downtown New York. Finally, we settled in a small, comfortably dark restaurant in the Village, at the choice window table. Even before the menu arrived, I noticed that my friend was uncomfortable. He was turning in his chair, peeking out of the window, looking distracted and concerned. On the other side of the street, in plain view, there was a brightly lit McDonald's in all its red and yellow glory. I made a decision immediately. "Do you want to go there, instead?" I asked. The friend eagerly leaped from his seat.

What is it about McDonald's that attracts children and immigrants alike? As a rule, immigrants, just like children, are very sensitive creatures. In their desire to blend in, they are conscious about making a wrong gesture, looking funny or different, standing out in any conspicuous way. The simple experience of entering a restaurant, asking for a table, and talking to a waiter can be intimidating. In this respect, McDonald's is the ultimate populist place. No one can be excluded—you can come and go as you please. It is OK to bring your children and to make a mess. Toys are given away, along with nutritional information: there is something for everyone.

The most important populist aspect of McDonald's is, of course, the food. Even though the American hamburger has been around since at least the beginning of the twentieth century, it did not catch up with the public imagination until the 1940s. At that time, America was obsessed with self-service. The wartime workforce was scarce and expensive, while mechanization had made a giant leap. The drive to cut labor as much as possible resulted in a rapid proliferation of self-service gas stations, department stores, cafeterias, and fast-food restaurants. It is not by chance the hamburger became

a staple of these new food establishments. American food was always characterized by meals composed of distinct elements. Instead of one-pot meals, so common in old Europe, American dinners historically had a tripartite structure: meat, potato, and vegetable. According to historian James Deetz, this difference points to a world view that places a greater emphasis on individuals and their free choice.

The fast food restaurants proposed a quite different trinity: hamburger, french fries, and soda. More important, however, were the separate, modular, and interchangeable elements that composed the entire meal. The inner structure of burger itself could easily be separated into further components, all open for inspection. The assembly of each hamburger has a clearly mechanical nature. Even the look of all parts alludes to various technological processes, rather than having a conventional appearance of cooked food. Thus, the beef patty is produced by molding, just like plastic parts, to a great degree of precision. (The diameter of a McDonald's burger is exactly 3.875 inches.) Fries are shaped, like aluminum extrusions, in precise square sections that have nothing to do with the shape of a potato. American cheese, itself a perfectly square yellow tile, is molded around the burger in a process that approximates thermo-forming. Only the bun still retains some resemblance to conventional bread, but even there, the precise slicing creates two matching parts similar to male-female parts of a mold. Individually added servings of ketchup play the role of oil and grease, necessary for the working of any mechanical assembly.

Ingredients of McDonald's

Much has been written about McDonald's development of special technologies that allowed the company to truly mechanize the fast-food business. Rarely noticed, however, is the fun component of all this necessary and unnecessary mechanization. There, in my opinion, lies a secret of McDonald's popularity, because Americans love to play with things industrial, mechanical, and technological. From children to adults, we enjoy having more video games, cars, telephones, and computers than any other nation in the world. American road restaurants contributed to this obsession by bringing technology and play into the realm of basic food consumption.

At the outset of the twenty-first century, in an age of theme restaurants, the idea of having fun while eating seems obvious. It was not so in 1948 when Richard and Mac McDonald started their enterprise. The image of a typical roadside restaurant at the time would be either faux-historical or cozily domestic. The spirit of the meal was, in general, about simplicity and efficiency. As such, it was a far cry from the romance of, say, a contemporary American car. McDonald's famous golden arches introduced a brave attempt to tie together architecture, food, and technology into one unified entertaining experience. The arches were the invention of Richard McDonald, who insisted on their incorporation into the new restaurant building. The story has it that several architects turned down his plan, not willing to deal with the "tasteless" client. Eventually, Stanley C. Meston, a local California architect, reluctantly accepted the commission. By the end of his work on the project, the arches assumed their characteristic parabolic shape. As it is often

"What's great about this country is that America started the tradition where the richest consumers buy essentially the same things as the poorest. A Coke is a Coke and no amount of money can get you a better Coke than the one the bum on the corner is drinking. All the Cokes are the same and all the Cokes are good."
—Andy Warhol, The Philosophy of Andy Warhol

Moscow McDonald's, 2000

noted, the curve most likely derived from Eero Saarinen's prize-winning St. Louis Arch, not yet built but widely published at the time. The interesting thing is that Saarinen's arch itself was probably influenced by a 1931 project, also unbuilt, by the great Le Corbusier. Yes, the first "golden arch" was proposed for Moscow, U.S.S.R., as a main compositional element for the giant Palace of the Soviets. The rest is history. Indeed, history is full of those improbable, ironic coincidences. Not only is the symbol of populist America derived from a high-Modernist architectural icon, but the ultimate capitalist machine of McDonald's is related to a palace for Communist Party congresses!

This connection became quite literal in the late 1980s, when newly liberalized Russia opened its doors to Western corporations. McDonald's was one of the first, and certainly the most noticeable, of the foreign companies who seized the opportunity right away. The site of the first Russian McDonald's was carefully chosen in the spiritual center of Moscow, across the street from the Pushkin monument. Even though it was reported to be the largest McDonald's restaurant in the world, the lines to get in stretched around the block during all possible hours and weather. Anecdotes circulated about business travelers who, after waiting in line for hours, would take the burger and fries (only one dinner was allowed per person) to their children far away in the provinces. After a long train journey, they would arrive days later to have the exotic food reheated and tasted by the whole family. Images of the McDonald's site with local crowds, policemen in uniform, or the Pushkin statue with the triumphant big "M" on the background became an obligatory part of any Western report about Russia in transition.

I visited the Moscow McDonald's a few years later, when the queues were long gone. It was evening, and the brightly lit place stood out even in its sumptuous Pushkin Square surroundings. The restaurant building was strangely attached to a conventional Soviet-style high rise, as if to permanently emphasize the existential collision of cultures. Driven by idle curiosity, I walked in and looked around. Surprisingly, the inside did not seem too different from the now familiar atmosphere of an American McDonald's. Families with children, groups of teenagers, people of all ages and financial means seemed busy and at ease. A young uniformed girl at the register addressed me not with the typical local "Next!" but with a Russian translation of "Can I help you?"—a new idiom that she was proud to say again and again. Suddenly, I felt at home. Yes, you can take McDonald's out of America, but you can't take America out of McDonald's.

Acknowledgements

The work featured in this book would not be possible without the contributions of the employees, interns, collaborators, and friends of Boym Studio. Nor would it happen without our clients, who entrusted us their projects and commissions. And it would certainly not be known without the journalists, writers, and editors who disseminated our designs and ideas around the world. To all of them, our thanks and acknowledgement.

To our employees and interns, past and present:
Christine Warren
Inna Alesina
Hlynur Vagn Atlason
Gina Aponte-Petrovich
Sang-Min Bae
Isabel Czerwenka-Wenkstetten
Michael Gordon
Jordan Kovin
John Lowe
Andrea Ruggiero
Heather Taylor
Ida Wanler

To our collaborators and contributors:
Miki Baytel
Meredith Beau
Alexander Gelman
Barbara Glauber/Heavy Meta
Lado Goudjabidze
Yvette Lenhart
Komar & Melamid
Jason Ring
Lloyd Schwan
Alex Valich
Marcel Wanders
Lev Zeitlin

Our special thanks go to Hjalti Karlsson and Jan Wilker, designers of the book, whose dedication, professionalism, and humor made the work one of those ideal collaborations you dream about.

We thank the contributors to the book, Peter Hall and, especially, Steven Skov Holt. On learning about our book, Steven rose to the challenge and was able to overcome his grave health problems to offer his inspiring essay on time.

We are grateful to George Tsypin for a casual summer discussion at the waterfall, which helped to formulate the concept of the book. Our thanks go to all friends who offered their opinions and advice: Paola Antonelli, Mel Byars, Maira Kalman, Vladimir Kanevsky, Lou Levine, Hans Maier-Aichen, Murray Moss, Stefan Sagmeister, Karim Rashid, Davira Taragin, and Tucker Viemeister. To Laurene's family, Maurice Leon and Martha Halperin, Lenore Leon, and Suzanne Leon; and to my dear parents in Moscow.

Our thanks go to Princeton Architectural Press—Kevin C. Lippert, publisher, Nettie Aljian, Ann Alter, Nicola Bednarek, Janet Behning, Penny Chu, Russell Fernandez, Mark Lamster, Nancy Eklund Later, Linda Lee, Jane Sheinman, Katharine Smalley, Scott Tennent, Jennifer Thompson, Deb Wood, and above all, to our editor, Clare Jacobson, whose friendly, energetic presence and support made the entire process of making a book such a pleasant experience.

Contributors:

PETER HALL is a writer and design critic based in New York. He is a contributing editor for *Metropolis* magazine and research fellow for the Design Institute at the University of Minnesota. He also teaches at Yale School of Art's MFA graphic design program. He wrote and co-edited the books *Tibor Kalman: Perverse Optimist* and *Sagmeister: Made You Look* and co-authored *Pause: 59 Minutes of Motion Graphics*.

STEVEN SKOV HOLT is a curious boy in his own right. He grew up in the rain forests of Connecticut, spent time in the urban jungles of New York, and then migrated to the foggy vistas of San Francisco. To pay for his bananas, tree house, and vine repair kit, he has worked with design firms and schools, including frogdesign (where he was both Visionary and VP of Creative Culture) and CCAC (where he is presently Chair of the Industrial Design program).

Photo credits:

The projects in this book cover our work from 1985 to 2002. We hope you continue following Boym Studio's future work—a lot more is cooking up. Please visit our website at www.boym.com and send us a message.

"From near to far
from here to there,
funny things are everywhere."
—Dr. Seuss

The End